LOSE WEIGHT ★ BE HEALTHY ★ EAS

D0253842

SUGAR BUST

For Life!

...WITH THE BRENNANS
PART II

COOKBOOK AND COMPANION GUIDE
Based on the diet principles found in
SUGAR BUSTERS!™ Cut Sugar To Trim Fat

ELLEN C. BRENNAN and THEODORE M. BRENNAN
of world-famous
BRENNAN'S RESTAURANT IN NEW ORLEANS
and co-authors of the best-selling cookbook
SUGAR BUST FOR LIFE!...WITH THE BRENNANS PART I

★ Over 300 New Recipes
★ Easy One-Dish Meals
★ Updated Shopper's Brand Name Guide
★ New Menus and Extensive Wine List
★ Weight Loss•Good Health "Tips For Success"

Ellen C. Brennan was the author of the Foreword,
Publishing Consultant, Distribution and Sales Coordinator for the
original *SUGAR BUSTERS™! Cut Sugar To Trim Fat*

OTHER BOOKS BY THE BRENNANS:

Breakfast at Brennan's and Dinner, Too

SUGAR BUST FOR LIFE!...WITH THE BRENNANS
Still available in book stores or through mail order (See page 321)
...also published as
SUGAR LESS FOR LIFE!...WITH THE BRENNANS

Published by Shamrock Publishing Inc.
P.O. Box 15439
New Orleans, Louisiana 70175-5439

Printed in the United States of America
Quebecor Printing Book Group

ISBN 0-9663519-2-4
Typography by Sir Speedy
First Edition

DEDICATION

To our loving family who with us persevered …

To our loyal friends who were always there for us …

To the myriads of well-wishers who came forth unexpectedly…

Collectively, their support and encouragement

throughout the *SUGAR BUST FOR LIFE!*

challenge further strengthened our commitment to help others –

and ultimately that made all the difference.

TABLE OF CONTENTS

ACKNOWLEDGMENTS

The successful publication of *SUGAR BUST FOR LIFE!...WITH THE BRENNANS, PART II* is attributed to several essential individuals. A big "thank you" to our two wonderful and talented daughters, Alana and Bridget, for their hand in a multitude of tasks well executed. A special "thank you" to our precious son, Teddy, for his endless suggestions.

Thank you to "Aunt" Barbara Heim, for facilitating the entire project in every way with the utmost perfection; and to GaGa, for her love and encouragement.

Thank you to the expert recipe creators and testers: Nicolle Hoy, Brennan's Restaurant Chef Michael Roussel and Sous Chef Lazone Randolph; and to Jimmy Brennan and Brennan's Restaurant cellar master, Harry Hill, for their excellent wine and champagne suggestions.

A big "thank you" also to Billie Cox, Wayne Chambless and everyone at Sir Speedy: Thank you, Billie, for your efficient and meticulous role in the production of *SUGAR BUST FOR LIFE!...WITH THE BRENNANS, PART II.*

INTRODUCTION

After Ellen C. Brennan's initial exposure to Michel Montignac's *Dine Out & Lose Weight* and her personal involvement with the original *SUGAR BUSTERS!™ Cut Sugar to Trim Fat*, she joined forces with her husband, Theodore M. Brennan, co-owner of Brennan's Restaurant in New Orleans and co-author of **Breakfast at Brennan's...and Dinner, Too,** to bring you *SUGAR BUST FOR LIFE!* The Brennans created an easy guide of recipes, menus, red wines and more, based on the Sugar Busters diet concept, to help weight loss while controlling diabetes and high cholesterol.

SUGAR BUST FOR LIFE!...WITH THE BRENNANS, PART II further provides the tools necessary in maintaining a healthful, low sugar lifestyle. *SUGAR BUST FOR LIFE!...WITH THE BRENNANS, PART II,* once again, responds to those in need of more information; scrumptious, yet, easy recipes, menus, an expanded brand name guide and tips for success in implementing the Sugar Busters diet.

As *SUGAR BUST FOR LIFE!...WITH THE BRENNANS, PART II* is not a medical guide, nor do its authors offer any medical advice, medical questions or concerns should be addressed to your physician. As in the original *SUGAR BUST FOR LIFE!,* the new *SUGAR BUST FOR LIFE! ... WITH THE BRENNANS, PART II* is written with firsthand knowledge of a low sugar lifestyle. It is a simplified guide to support your change in eating habits.

Surrounded by dining opportunities, Ellen and Ted Brennan understand the challenge. Without sacrificing three scrumptious meals and satisfying snacks every day, the Brennans have wisely adjusted their eating habits to maintain their good health—and you can, too! *SUGAR BUST FOR LIFE!...WITH THE BRENNANS, PART II* provides a low sugar way of eating without relying on counting calories or fat grams. There is no guesswork in making wise choices.

Ellen and Ted Brennan have mastered a simple, healthful low sugar lifestyle, while indulging in culinary creations that satisfy the most discriminating palates. Once again, they have compiled a perfect cookbook and companion guide for the new millennium—*SUGAR BUST FOR LIFE!...WITH THE BRENNANS, PART II.*

FOOD GUIDE

SUGAR BUST FOR LIFE!...WITH THE BRENNANS, PART II reveals everything you will need to achieve an easy, low sugar lifestyle. Simply know that there are foods you can eat, foods you cannot eat and foods to be eaten in moderation. Let the following lists be your easy guide as you *SUGAR BUST FOR LIFE!...WITH THE BRENNANS.*

Foods for Feasting

Low Glycemic Foods
0–40 Index

Meats and Fowl, lean and skinless

Alligator	Pork
Beef	Quail
Chicken	Rabbit
Cornish Hens	Squab
Duck	Turkey
Goose	Veal
Lamb	Venison
Liver	Other Wild Game

Seafood

Abalone	Mussels
Anchovies	Oysters
Catfish	Pompano
Caviar	Prawns
Clams	Redfish
Cod	Red Snapper
Crabmeat	Salmon
Crawfish	Sardines
Drum	Scallops
Eel	Sea Bass
Flounder	Shark
Grouper	Shrimp
Haddock	Snails
Halibut	Sole
Herring	Squid
Lemon Fish	Swordfish
Mackeral	Trout
Lobster	Tuna
Mahi Mahi	Turbot

Dairy Products

Butter	Eggs
Cheeses, assorted	Margarine
Cottage Cheese	Milk, all types
Cream	Sour Cream
Cream Cheese	Yogurt

Note: The sugar found in milk is a natural sugar called lactose which is acceptable.

Vegetables

Alfalfa Sprouts	Kale
Artichokes	Kidney or Red Beans
Arugula	Leeks
Asparagus	Lettuce
Avocado	Lima Beans
Bamboo Shoots	Mint
Bean Sprouts	Mirliton
Black Beans	Mushrooms
Broccoli	Mustard Greens
Brussel Sprouts	Okra
Butter Beans	Onions
Cabbage	Parsley
Cauliflower	Radicchio
Celery	Radishes
Chick Peas	Red Bell Peppers
Chili Peppers	Red Peppers
Collard Greens	Scallions
Cucumbers	Shallots
Eggplant	Soy Beans
Endives	Spinach
Escarole	Squash, Yellow
Fennel	Tomatoes
Garbanzo Beans	Turnips
Garlic	Turnip Greens
Green Beans	Watercress
Green Onions	Water Chestnuts
Green Bell Peppers	Yellow Bell Peppers
Hearts of Palm	Zucchini
Jalapeno Peppers	

Miscellaneous

Beverages (free of sugar or other unacceptable ingredients)

Brown Rice Cakes

Chocolate
(60% or greater cocoa content)

Coffee

Cooking Oils (Canola, Corn, Olive, Peanut, Safflower, Soybean, etc.)

Dill Pickles

Hot Sauces

Mustards

Nuts

Olives

Peanut Butter

Seasonings and Spices

Sauerkraut

Soy Products

Soy Sauce

Tea

Tofu, fresh (read label)

Vinegar

Fresh Fruit

The glycemic index of each fruit listed ranges from low to moderate.

Apples

Apricots

Blackberries

Blueberries

Boysenberries

Cantaloupe

Cherries

Cranberries

Figs

Grapefruit

Grapes

Honeydew Melon

Lemons

Limes

Manderin Oranges

Nectarines

Oranges

Papaya

Peaches

Pears

Persimmon

Plantains

Pomegranate

Plums

Raspberries

Satsumas

Strawberries

Tangerines

The sugar found in fruit is a natural sugar called fructose. It is only detrimental to the low sugar way of life when eaten at the wrong time or with other food groups.

- The rule to apply with no exception is the following: Fruit must be consumed alone at least 30 minutes prior to eating anything else or at least 2 hours after eating.

- Natural whole fruit preserves with no sugar added should be eaten the same way as fresh fruit. However, an occasional treat of an acceptable cracker with sugarless whole fruit preserves is not harmful.

- Fruit juice, even unsweetened, is quickly absorbed when consumed. The minimum pulp content of fruit juice as compared to the rich pulp content in a piece of fruit can create an intense glycemic response — that is, fruit juice can elevate blood sugar levels. We believe that fruit juice, even unsweetened, should be avoided for weight reduction or for blood sugar level maintenance. Once desired weight is attained and if glycemic response is not a serious concern, the consumption of fruit juice should follow the same rule applied to fruit — that is at least 30 minutes prior to a meal or at least 2 hours after.

- Sugar free desserts containing fruit are not included in the "Just Dessert" recipe section. However, we believe the use of lemon and lime juice in our recipes to be insignificant and the rule for fruit consumption to be non-applicable. A sugar free fruit dessert should follow the same rule for consumption as any fresh fruit — that is 30 minutes before a meal or at least 2 hours after. The demand for desserts with such a restriction is limited. In addition, a sugar free fruit dessert should consist only of the fruit itself and should not include other ingredients such as cereal, cottage cheese, cream, cream cheese, eggs, ice cream, nuts, ricotta cheese, sour cream, whipped toppings, pie crusts (even whole grain), yogurt, etc.

Foods for Moderation

Moderate Glycemic Foods
40 – 60 Index

Whole Grain Breads, Flours and Pasta

Mixed Whole Grain Breads
Oat Bran Bread
Pumpernickel Bread
Rye Bread
Stone Ground Whole Wheat Bread
Stone Ground Whole Wheat Pita Bread
Whole Grain Flours (Barley, Brown Rice, Oat, Rye,
Stone Ground Whole Wheat, etc.)
Stone Ground Whole Wheat Pasta
100% Whole Durum Wheat Semolina Pasta

Vegetables

Black-eyed Peas	Pinto Beans
Green Peas	Split Peas
Lentils	Sweet Potatoes
Navy Beans	Yams

Whole Grains

Barley	Oat Bran
Brown Basmati Rice	Oatmeal
Brown Rice	Wheat Bran
Buckwheat	Wheat Germ
Bulgar	Whole Grain Cereal
Cracked Wheat	Wild Rice

Forbidden Foods

High Glycemic Foods
60 and greater index

Fruits & Vegetables

Bananas

Beets

Carrots

Corn

Dates

Kiwi, very ripe

Mango

Parsnips

Pineapple

Potatoes, Red and White

Prunes

Raisins

Taro

Watermelon

Snacks

Candy

Chee Wheez

Chocolate (less than 60% cocoa content)

Corn Chips

Cornnuts

French Fries

Granola Bars

Ice Cream (most), Ice Milk, Sherbet, Sorbets and Other Frozen Desserts

Museli Bars

Popcorn

Potato Chips and Sticks

Pretzels

Rice Cakes

Baked Goods, Flours & Grains

Bagels, Wheat and White	French Bread
Biscuits, Wheat and White	Gingerbread
Bread, Wheat and White	Grits
Bread Crumbs	Hamburger and Hot Dog Buns
Breadsticks	Kaiser Rolls
Bread Stuffing	Melba Toast
Cakes	Millet
Cereals, Refined	Muffins
Cookies	Pancakes
Corn Bread	Pastries
Corn Flour	Pies
Cornmeal	Pita Bread
Couscous	Pizza
Cracker Meal	Refined White Pasta
Crackers, Wheat and White	Rice, Basmati White
Cream of Wheat	Rice, Instant (Even Brown)
Croissants	Rice, White
Croutons	Shortbread
Donuts	Taco Shells
English Muffin	Tapioca
Flour, Enriched Wheat† and White	Waffles

 BEWARE: Many sugar free baked goods are unacceptable because they are made with refined wheat flour and not stone ground whole wheat flour.

†Do not confuse wheat flour with stone ground whole wheat flour. However, as noted on the label most brand name stone ground whole wheat breads are laced with "hidden sugars" such as honey.

Beverages

Beer (Includes Ale and Lite Beer)
Chocolate and Malted Milk Drinks
Colas and Drinks: bottled, canned and packaged mixtures (containing sugar, hidden sugars or other unacceptable ingredients)
Liqueurs
Tonic Water

Miscellaneous

Barbecue Sauce

Breakfast Bars, Drinks and Pastries

Chili Sauce

Coffee Creamers

Condensed Milk

Fruit Jams, Jellies and Preserves

Gelatin Mixes, Flavored and Sweetened

Gravy (Canned and Packaged)

Hamburger Mix

Ketchup (Most)

Marshmallows

Meal Supplements

Meat spreads, canned

Pot Pies, Frozen

Prepared Meals (Canned, Frozen and Packaged)

Pudding Mixes

Salad Dressings (Many Bottled and Most Packaged)

Soups (Most Canned and Packaged)

Tofu (read label — beware of unacceptable ingredients)

Tofu Non-Dairy Frozen Dessert

Tofu Ice Cream

Hidden Sugar & Other Unacceptable Ingredients

Barley Malt	Honey
Beet Juice	Malted Barley
Beet Sugar	Maltodextrin
Brown Rice Syrup	Maltose
Brown Sugar	Maple Syrup
Cane Juice	Modified Food Starch
Cane Syrup	Modified Tapioca Starch
Cornstarch	Molasses
Corn Syrup	Potato Starch
Dextrose	Raisin Juice
Flour: Corn, Enriched Wheat and White	Sugar, Raw and Refined
Glucose	Sucrose
High Fructose Corn Syrup	

WEIGHT LOSS•GOOD HEALTH
"TIPS FOR SUCCESS"

SUGAR BUST FOR LIFE!...WITH THE BRENNANS, PART II is the answer to less than satisfying meals and restrictive low calorie diets that for some people even create a fear of food. Such deprivation is not good for your well-being. You will learn to enjoy eating and still be healthy as you *SUGAR BUST FOR LIFE!...WITH THE BRENNANS* throughout the new millennium. This new way of life will help you lose weight and keep it off without feeling hungry or craving food for long periods of time.

First and foremost, it is important to understand that refined or simple sugar and certain complex carbohydrates known as high glycemic carbohydrates are harmful to your health and stimulate the pancreas to secrete high levels of insulin. Insulin regulates blood sugar levels. High levels of insulin cause storage of excess sugar, not used for energy, as fat, inducing the liver to produce cholesterol.

Excessive consumption of refined sugar and other high glycemic carbohydrates can affect the immune system and create the risk for disease. *SUGAR BUST FOR LIFE!...WITH THE BRENNANS, PART II* can improve cholesterol, triglycerides, blood sugar levels, blood pressure, digestive disorders, help attain that desired weight while diminishing the symptoms of diabetes and restoring strength and stamina.

The following "tips for success" are meant to simplify your low sugar lifestyle and facilitate its maintenance:

1) The *SUGAR BUST FOR LIFE!* way of eating is not about counting fat grams or calories but about simply avoiding refined sugar and other high glycemic carbohydrates.

2) This is not a quick weight loss concept. Yet, weight loss should be steady and consistent by eating from all food groups in moderation.

3) Remember the key words—Moderation and Portion Control—coupled with the fact that no two people are exactly alike. Telling you to eat only a certain number of calories or fat grams daily is not the answer. Reasonably sized servings are a "must." There is no set formula for everyone. What works for you should be determined and modified by the individual. Most importantly, it is necessary to exercise caution in

the quantity of food you consume despite the fact your mother may have taught you to eat everything on your plate.

4) Finding what is exactly right for you is accomplished by trial and error. Once your desired weight is attained, a maintenance plan should be easily determined by the same trial and error method.

5) Many people are guilty of overeating the "right" foods! The over-consumption of moderate glycemic carbohydrates, such as whole grain pasta, brown rice, beans, sweet potatoes, whole grain breads,* as well as whole grain cereals** can cause weight loss to stop or slow down. If this happens, try restricting yourself to protein and green vegetables for a while to achieve better results and, cautiously, ease in the moderate glycemic carbohydrates once weight loss resumes.

*Caution especially should be exercised in the consumption of whole grain bread. More than one slice a day can inhibit weight loss for many.
**Shredded Wheat has a borderline high glycemic index and should be consumed only occasionally if at all.

6) Some people have realized that weight loss is expedited by eating protein alone. Interestingly, eating protein alone has the directly opposite effect of eating the high glycemic carbohydrates that are stored as fat. Therefore, eating just a sirloin strip, a grilled chicken breast or Flounder with lemon butter sauce will signal the pancreas, instead, to secrete an enzyme called glucagon which, actually, will break down stored fat.

7) Michel Montignac, the French weight loss guru and primary source for the Sugar Busters diet, believed the following to be very significant: Eating meals of moderate glycemic carbohydrates (with or without green vegetables) separately from meals consisting of proteins and fats (with or without green vegetables) should promote weight loss.

8) You will find that eating low glycemic foods will leave you feeling full for longer periods of time compared to eating high glycemic foods.

9) It is never wise to eat right before going to bed. Be sure to eat no later than three hours before bedtime. Most cholesterol is produced at night and a late night meal can cause indigestion.

10) Meals should be well-balanced with all food groups eaten in moderation

and that includes fat. Beware, however, that some fats are bad and others are not! Saturated fats can increase your blood cholesterol level or low-density lipoproteins (LDL), known as "bad" cholesterol. On the other hand, monounsaturated fats such as olive, canola and fish oils can be good for you as they should not adversely effect your high-density lipoproteins (HDL) or "good" cholesterol and can actually elevate HDL levels.

11) The consumption of the necessary 20-25 grams of fiber daily is essential.

12) In our recipes, there is opportunity for you to modify your fat intake by choosing skim milk over cream, margarine over butter, olive oil over other oils. This is not a high fat diet as some might think. All food groups are to be eaten in moderation. You control what and how much you eat. *SUGAR BUST FOR LIFE!...WITH THE BRENNANS* is about eating healthily with moderation as the key.

13) For the person "on the go," forethought and advance preparation of lunch is most helpful for achieving set goals. Packing a lunch bag of fruit and cheese with a chicken breast, a container of tuna salad atop mixed greens or half of a sandwich are just a few ideas for viable substitutes for any menu lunch item.

14) Any of the suggested dinner menus may be eaten midday instead. Some people may prefer the luncheon items as a light evening fare.

15) It is best to eat three balanced meals and three snacks every day. Snacks during the day can actually be good for you because they keep your blood sugar from dropping too low and your metabolism from slowing down.

16) If fruit is your snack, remember its rule at all times. Fruit should be eaten alone, at least thirty minutes prior to a meal or at least two hours after a meal.

17) Even if you fall prey to small amounts of "forbidden" foods, no permanent harm is done. You simply modify your next meals accordingly to get back on track.

18) Read packaging of all foods carefully. Refer to page 271 to learn how to read a label. For example, beware of breads and cereals—most are laced with sugar, honey or molasses.

19) Women sometimes complain that they don't lose weight as easily as men. Again, this is where trial and error methods may come into place. Women may need to be more aware than men of portion control and more cautious about carbohydrate consumption, especially those moderate glycemic carbohydrates. Once again, the elimination of such carbohydrates at certain meals and a regimen of protein and green vegetables only should expedite weight loss. Perhaps, eating protein alone at lunch or dinner for a period of time would be beneficial.

20) Weight loss in women also can be stymied by hormones or birth control pills. So, if you are a woman who is taking these types of medication, by all means, check with your physician.

21) Drinking eight glasses of water daily is very important.

22) Limiting your sodium intake is also important. Drinking an adequate amount of water helps to eliminate excess sodium from your body.

23) Drinking too much of anything during a meal interferes with digestion.

24) Sugar free beverages with caffeine are acceptable in moderation. Just beware that caffeine is a stimulant and will cultivate your appetite. Some sugar free beverages are also high in sodium.

25) Remember, too, that alcoholic beverages can inhibit any diet. If you choose to indulge, remember never to do so on an empty stomach and extreme moderation should be exercised in its consumption. Red and white wines, particularly dry ones, as well as champagne and hard liquors, if mixed with anything sugar free, are all acceptable alcoholic beverages. Drinking a glass of red wine daily can actually benefit your cardiac health and can also be instrumental in lowering "bad" (LDL) cholesterol levels while raising the "good" (HDL) ones.

26) Last but not least, exercise daily to benefit your overall health. Again, check with your physician as to the best type of exercise for you. Yes! You are eating adequate carbohydrates for exercise unless, that is, you are a marathon runner. Remember, fruit and vegetables have natural sugars and this is a low sugar dietary concept, not a no sugar dietary concept. Only strictly protein diets can cause ketosis.

Easy is what *SUGAR BUST FOR LIFE!...WITH THE BRENNANS* is about—an easy road to a healthful new life for you!

FOURTEEN
DAILY MENUS

As you *SUGAR BUST FOR LIFE!* throughout the new millennium, these fourteen daily menus will help you maintain your low sugar lifestyle with very little guesswork. Remember these are only suggested menus. Substitution at any meal of a different recipe or one of your own creation is acceptable. Luncheon and dinner items are interchangeable and changing the order or eliminating an item altogether is also acceptable.

The versatility and creativity of the menus in *SUGAR BUST FOR LIFE!...WITH THE BRENNANS, PART II* will help you implement your new and healthy way of life. You will eat well as you *SUGAR BUST FOR LIFE!*

WEEK 1

MONDAY	BREAKFAST	LUNCH	DINNER
	¹/₂ Honeydew Melon (wait 30 minutes) Puffed Kashi With Skim Milk Sugar Free Yogurt Coffee or Tea	Chilled Avocado Soup (Page 63) Beef Burritos With Lettuce Wraps (Page 141)	Cucumber & Radish Salad (Page 87) Chicken Pecan (Page 176) Wild Rice and Peas (Page 236)
	Snack (Page 18)	Snack (Page 18)	Snack (Page 18)
TUESDAY	BREAKFAST	LUNCH	DINNER
	¹/₂ Grapefruit (wait 30 minutes) Scrambled Egg 1 Slice Canadian Bacon Stone Ground Whole Wheat Toast With Butter, Margarine or Cream Cheese Coffee or Tea	Brussels Sprouts With Dill Dressing (Page 87) Shrimp Aegean (Page 127)	Italian Tomato Salad (Page 91) Veal Scallopini (Page 185) Red Pepper Green Beans (Page 229)
	Snack (Page 18)	Snack (Page 18)	Snack (Page 18)
WEDNESDAY	BREAKFAST	LUNCH	DINNER
	Blackberries (wait 30 minutes) Oatmeal Sugar Free Yogurt Coffee or Tea	Broccoli Vegetable Soup (Page 65) Turkey Salad Vinaigrette (Page103)	Tossed Green Salad With Lemon Mustard Vinaigrette (Page 110) Shrimp With Dill (Page 169) Spinach Au Gratin (Page 233)
	Snack (Page 18)	Snack (Page 18)	Snack (Page 18)
THURSDAY	BREAKFAST	LUNCH	DINNER
	Orange (wait 30 minutes) Pumpernickel or Rye Toast With Butter or Margarine and Melted Cheese Sugar Free Yogurt Coffee or Tea	Maude's Table Side Salad (Page 99) Parmesan Dijon Chicken (Page 132)	Greek Tomato Salad (Page 90) Baked Salmon With Fresh Basil (Page 164) Zucchini With Fresh Mint (Page 234)
	Snack (Page 18)	Snack (Page 18)	Snack (Page 18)

FRIDAY	BREAKFAST	LUNCH	DINNER
	Strawberries (wait 30 minutes) Uncle Sam Cereal With Skim Milk Sugar Free Yogurt Coffee or Tea	Tossed Green Salad With Basil Mint Vinaigrette (Page 114) Garlic Chicken (Page 171)	Steamed Artichokes (Page 84) Tedito's Margherita Pizza (Page 212)
	Snack (Page 18)	Snack (Page 18)	Snack (Page 18)
SATURDAY	BREAKFAST	LUNCH	DINNER
	Peach (wait 30 minutes) Poached Egg atop Canadian Bacon and Stone Ground Whole Wheat Toast or Sweet Potato and Chicken Breakfast Hash (Page 138) Coffee or Tea	Tomato and Mushroom Soup (Page 70) Shrimp and Pasta Salad (Page 106)	Green Beans and Feta Salad (Page 89) Leg of Lamb (Page 183) Crème Fraiche Sweet Potatoes (Page 240) Mini Peanut Butter Chocolate Pies (Page 251)
	Snack (Page 18)	Snack (Page 18)	Snack (Page 18)
SUNDAY	BREAKFAST	LUNCH	DINNER
	½ Cantaloupe (wait 30 minutes) Almond Oatmeal Waffle (Page 157) With Butter or Margarine and Sugar Free Maple Syrup or Shrimp Omelette (Page 149) With Whole Wheat Ginger Muffins (Page 253) Coffee or Tea	Cream of Crab Soup (Page 77) Rex Salad (Page 100)	Tossed Green Salad With Red Wine Vinaigrette (Page 116) Veal Chops Dijon (Page 185) Squash au Gratin (Page 231)
	Snack (Page 18)	Snack (Page 18)	Snack (Page 18)

WEEK 2

MONDAY	BREAKFAST	LUNCH	DINNER
	Apple (wait 30 minutes) Puffed Kashi With Skim Milk Sugar Free Yogurt Coffee or Tea	Cold Cucumber Bisque (Page 67) Grilled Chicken Caesar Salad (Page 130)	Avocado With Gorgonzola Dressing (Page 86) Blackeyed Peas (Page 144) Brown Rice (Page 239)
	Snack (Page 18)	Snack (Page 18)	Snack (Page 18)
TUESDAY	BREAKFAST	LUNCH	DINNER
	Plum (wait 30 minutes) Scrambled Egg Stone Ground Whole Wheat Toast With Butter or Margarine Sugar Free Sausage Coffee or Tea	Cream of Mushroom & Onion Soup (Page 69) New York Deli Salad (Page 102)	Vegetable Salad (Page 92) Chicken Madrid (Page 175) Pasta With Cheese & Herbs (Page 196)
	Snack (Page 18)	Snack (Page 18)	Snack (Page 18)
WEDNESDAY	BREAKFAST	LUNCH	DINNER
	1/2 Cantaloupe (wait 30 minutes) Oatmeal Sugar Free Yogurt Coffee or Tea	Broccoli and Celery Salad (Page 86) Shrimp Salad Wraps (Page 128)	Tossed Green Salad With Dijon Parmesan Dressing (Page 109) Turkey Sloppy Joes (Page 182) Herbed Stove Top Brown Rice (Page 238)
	Snack (Page 18)	Snack (Page 18)	Snack (Page 18)
THURSDAY	BREAKFAST	LUNCH	DINNER
	1/2 Grapefruit (wait 30 minutes) Kellogg's Extra Fiber All Bran Coffee or Tea	Cream of Asparagus Soup (Page 62) Hot Beef Salad (Page 101)	Athen's Salad (Page 90) Salmon With Dill Sauce (Page 163) Peas & Mushrooms (Page 230)
	Snack (Page 18)	Snack (Page 18)	Snack (Page 18)

FRIDAY	**BREAKFAST**	**LUNCH**	**DINNER**
	Blueberries (wait 30 minutes) Uncle Sam Cereal With Skim Milk Sugar Free Yogurt Coffee or Tea	Tossed Green Salad With Garlic Dressing (Page 107) Tampico Shrimp & Black Bean Chili (Page 126)	Wild Rice Salad (Page 104) Roasted Chicken (Page 171) Sauteed Broccoli (Page 224)
	Snack (Page 18)	Snack (Page 18)	Snack (Page 18)
SATURDAY	**BREAKFAST**	**LUNCH**	**DINNER**
	½ Cantaloupe (wait 30 minutes) Egg, Sunny Side Up or Once Over Easy 1 Strip Bacon Stone Ground Whole Wheat Toast With Butter or Margarine or Sweet Potato Pancakes (Page 156) With Butter or Margarine and Sugar Free Maple Syrup Coffee or Tea	Avocado & Dill Soup (Page 64) Blackened Redfish Salad (Page 129)	Garlic Salad (Page 98) French Pork Cutlets (Page 183) Baked Sweet Potatoes With Blue Cheese (Page 241) Chocolate Mint Souflé (Page 256)
	Snack (Page 18)	Snack (Page 18)	Snack (Page 18)
SUNDAY	**BREAKFAST**	**LUNCH**	**DINNER**
	Strawberries (wait 30 minutes) Corned Beef and Swiss Cheese Quiche (Page 154) or Canadian Bacon With Whole Wheat Cheese Biscuits (Page 261) Coffee or Tea	Green Beans & Tomato Salad (Page 89) Red Pepper Shrimp (Page 170)	Tossed Green Salad With Classical French Dressing (Page 107) Fat Harry's Pizza (Page 221)
	Snack (Page 18)	Snack (Page 18)	Snack (Page 18)

SUGGESTED SNACKS

Assorted Cheeses

Baba Ghannouge Dip with acceptable
crackers or raw vegetables

Cheese Spreads and acceptable crackers

Chocolate – a square of 60%
or greater cocoa content
(with a few of your favorite nuts gives
the taste of a candy bar!)

Cottage Cheese

Creole Cream Cheese

Deviled or Hard-Boiled Egg

Dill Pickles

Dips, Spreads and Tapenades with Raw
Vegetables or Crackers

Feta Spreads with acceptable crackers
or raw vegetables

Fruit (to be eaten 30 minutes before a
meal or at least 2 hours after a meal)

Green Salad with dressing

Guacamole with Triscuit

Hot Chocolate (60% or greater cocoa)

Hummus with acceptable crackers or
raw vegetables

Jell-O Sugar Free Low Calorie
Gelatin Snacks

Lentil Chips

Nuts (plain, roasted or spiced)

Olives (black, green, Kalamata
or stuffed)

Peanut Butter or other flavored butters
on celery or acceptable crackers

Pickled or Marinated Vegetables (cauliflower, green beans, okra, etc.)

Pumpkin Seeds (plain, curry and chili
flavored)

Raw Vegetables
(plain, with cheese spread, cream
cheese, peanut butter or dip)

Brown Rice Cake with Peanut Butter or
Other Spread

Sardines and Sliced Onions

Smoked Clams and Oysters

Soup

Stone Ground Whole Wheat Pretzels
with Peanut Butter

Sweet Potato Chips

Sweet Potato Sticks with Almonds,
Cashews or Peanuts

Tahini with crackers or raw vegetables

Triscuit Nachos (Triscuit with melted
cheese, salsa and jalapeno peppers)

Yogurt, Sugar-free

18

RECIPES "WORDS TO THE WISE"

Ellen and Ted Brennan have mastered the easy, healthful lifestyle of *SUGAR BUST FOR LIFE!* With many dining opportunities, Ellen and Ted understand the challenge and the difficulties of following a low sugar way of life as well as the difficulties of abiding by most weight loss programs. In particular, they recognize the torment in resisting favorite foods as well as the associated guilt and dread of excess pounds.

Unlike other diets, which restrict calorie or fat gram intake, while creating less than satisfying meals and downright unbearable hunger pangs, *SUGAR BUST FOR LIFE!* alleviates these problems. *SUGAR BUST FOR LIFE!...WITH THE BRENNANS, PART II* provides a healthy meal plan without sacrificing easy and delicious meals for every day of the week.

Some recipes should be prepared in advance to facilitate the preparation of recipes. In particular, barbecue sauce, ketchup, mayonnaise, salad dressings, and ice cream should be prepared ahead of time to reduce your time spent in the kitchen. This extra prep time will simplify preparation of many recipes for all meals and, in particular, will expedite, an oftentimes, hurried dinner hour.

In the original *SUGAR BUST FOR LIFE!...WITH THE BRENNANS,* Sweet 'N Low® was used in the recipes, as it does not lose its sweetness with

19

heat, in particular, while baking. Also Sweet 'N Low® was the artificial sweetener of choice as the Brennans found that it creates less of an aftertaste.

However, in *SUGAR BUST FOR LIFE!...WITH THE BRENNANS, PART II,* the use of two new, natural sugar substitutes is recommended. *Ki-Sweet* is the sweetener of choice by the Brennans in their dessert recipes. It is an all natural, low glycemic sweetener made from kiwi fruit and invented by Dr. Ann de Wees Allen, N.D. of the Glycemic Research Institute in Washington, D.C. You will appreciate how well it sweetens while cooking or baking. *Ki-Sweet* is available online at *http://www.anndeweesallen.com* or by calling *Nutrition For Life International* at 1-888-688-6354 or by visiting *http://www.nutritionforlife.com.*

The Brennans also suggest another new, natural sweetener, the herb *Stevia.* Although not used in their recipes, this excellent sweetener may be found in health food stores. Both of these suggested new, natural sugar substitutes are highly recommended. It is believed that they do not have the adverse side effects of many commonly used artificial sweeteners.

According to the Brennans' experience, the following sugar equivalents should be a helpful guide:

5 teaspoons sugar = $^1/_3$ teaspoon *Ki-Sweet* = $^2/_3$ teaspoon *Sweet 'N Low*®

$^1/_4$ cup sugar = $^3/_4$ teaspoon *Ki-Sweet* = $1^1/_2$ teaspoons *Sweet 'N Low*®

$^1/_2$ cup sugar = $1^1/_2$ teaspoons *Ki-Sweet* = 3 teaspoons *Sweet 'N Low*®

1 cup sugar = 3 teaspoons *Ki-Sweet* = 6 teaspoons *Sweet 'N Low*®

You will find that the recipe section includes various pasta, pizza, rice and sweet potato suggestions. Forever be cautious not to overeat the "right" foods. Although certain recipes call for brown rice, stone ground whole wheat flour, sweet potatoes and whole grain pasta, over-consumption of these moderate glycemic carbohydrates can cause weigh loss to stop or slow down. Unless your desired weight is attained, the aforementioned foods should not be your main meal but an occasional side dish. As always, moderation is key.

In the recipes, there is opportunity for you to modify your fat intake by choosing skim or low fat milk over cream, margarine over butter, canola or olive oil over other oils. *Exercise caution as many times low and no fat equate to high sugar content.* However, this is not a high fat diet as some might think. Food groups are to be eaten in moderation with you controlling what you eat.

Just keep in mind that suggested low fat modifications will alter the consistency of soups and sauces making them thin in texture. Instead of using cream, white flour or cornstarch as a thickener, substitute 2 tablespoons of stone ground whole wheat flour, which is equivalent to the same amount of white flour or to 1 tablespoon of cornstarch. Be sure to strain the sauce before serving for a smooth consistency.

The following guide will help you modify your fat intake if you so choose:

Low Fat Modifications

Whole Milk	*instead use*	Skim, Low fat, Buttermilk
Heavy Cream	*instead use*	Evaporated Skim Milk
Butter	*instead use*	Margarine, Olive or Canola Oil
Sour Cream	*instead use*	Low fat sour cream or Light Yogurt
Whipped Cream	*instead use*	Chilled & Whipped Evaporated Skim Milk with a dash of lemon juice
High Fat Cheese	*instead use*	Skim Milk Cheese
Cream Cheese	*instead use*	Neufchatel Cheese
Egg	*instead use*	2 Egg Whites or ¼ cup Egg Substitute
Mayonnaise	*instead use*	Light Yogurt
Bacon	*instead use*	Lean Ham or Canadian Bacon
Ice Cream	*instead use*	Sugar free Fruit Flavored Ice
Salad Dressing	*instead use*	Olive Oil with Vinegar or Lemon

The new recipes included in *SUGAR BUST FOR LIFE!...WITH THE BRENNANS PART II* will create more opportunities for fine dining from your very own kitchen. The days of monotonous, unsatisfying dieting are over. For your culinary pleasure, the Brennans' recipes offer fine quality and flavor. You will eat healthy while satisfying the most discriminating palates.

APPETIZERS
AND PARTY FOOD

FRESH AVOCADO DIP

3 ripe avocados, peeled and pitted
1 garlic clove
½ cup medium salsa
2 teaspoons fresh lemon juice
4 teaspoons dried cilantro
½ teaspoon salt
¼ teaspoon black pepper
1 medium tomato, chopped

Serves four to six

Combine all ingredients, except tomato, in a food processor until smooth. Place the dip in a serving bowl, and top with the chopped tomato. Serve with celery, green peppers, asparagus, and broccoli or an acceptable cracker (see Brand Name Guide).

BACON AND TOMATO DIP

10 slices bacon, cooked until crisp, and cooled
3 large tomatoes, chopped
1 cup mayonnaise (see Index)
1 tablespoon Dijon mustard
¼ cup green onion, minced
¼ cup fresh parsley, minced
2 dashes Tabasco®

Serves four to six

Combine all ingredients in a food processor until smooth. Place the dip in a serving bowl, cover, and refrigerate for 2 hours. Serve with celery, green peppers, asparagus, and broccoli or an acceptable cracker (see Brand Name Guide).

ROQUEFORT CHEESE DIP

12 oz. cream cheese, room temperature

½ cup butter or margarine, softened

1 tablespoon paprika

1½ teaspoons caraway seeds

¾ cup Roquefort cheese, room temperature

2 dashes Tabasco®

Serves four to six

Combine all ingredients in a food processor until smooth. Place the dip in a serving bowl, cover, and refrigerate for 2 hours. Serve with celery, green peppers, asparagus, and broccoli or an acceptable cracker (see Brand Name Guide).

CHEDDAR AND CAPER DIP

8 oz. sharp Cheddar cheese, room temperature

8 oz. cream cheese, room temperature

3 tablespoons capers, chopped

1 teaspoon caraway seeds

¾ cup sour cream

2 tablespoons onion, chopped

1 teaspoon black pepper

Serves four to six

Combine all ingredients in a food processor until smooth. Place the dip in a serving bowl and serve with celery, green peppers, asparagus, and broccoli or an acceptable cracker (see Brand Name Guide).

BOSTON CRABMEAT DIP

8 oz. cream cheese, room temperature

1 tablespoon milk

1 lb. lump crabmeat

2 tablespoons onion, chopped

1½ teaspoons horseradish

¼ teaspoon salt

2 tablespoons sherry

Preheat oven to 350° F.

Serves eight

Mix the cream cheese and the milk; then add other ingredients and mix well. Place in a small baking dish and cover. Bake for 20 to 30 minutes. Serve with acceptable crackers (see Brand Name Guide).

SPRING GARDEN DIP

1 cup plain yogurt

1 cup sour cream

1 large cucumber, peeled and chopped

4 garlic cloves, minced

1½ teaspoons dried mint leaves

3 tablespoons olive oil

4 teaspoons red wine vinegar

½ teaspoon onion powder

Serves four to six

Combine all ingredients in a food processor until smooth. Place the dip in a serving bowl, cover, and refrigerate for 2 hours. Serve with celery, green peppers, asparagus, and broccoli or an acceptable cracker (see Brand Name Guide).

FRESH HERB DIP

12 oz. cream cheese, room temperature

1 cup sour cream

¼ cup green onion, chopped

2 tablespoons fresh parsley, chopped

1 teaspoon salt

¼ teaspoon cayenne pepper

1 garlic clove, minced

1 tablespoon fresh tarragon, chopped

1 teaspoon fresh lemon juice

3 teaspoons capers

Serves four to six

Combine all ingredients in a food processor until smooth. Place the dip in a serving bowl, cover, and refrigerate for 2 hours. Serve with celery, green peppers, asparagus, and broccoli or an acceptable cracker (see Brand Name Guide).

HUMMUS

15 oz. canned garbanzo beans, rinsed and drained

¼ cup lemon juice

4 garlic cloves, minced

½ teaspoon salt

¼ teaspoon paprika

3 tablespoons tahini

2 tablespoons fresh parsley, chopped

3 tablespoons olive oil

Serves four to six

Combine all ingredients in a food processor until smooth. Add additional olive oil as necessary to make a smooth, light paste. Serve with acceptable crackers (see Brand Name Guide).

SANTA FE SALSA

4 medium tomatoes, finely chopped

1 small onion, finely chopped

2 jalapeno peppers, finely chopped

2 tablespoons fresh cilantro, chopped

1 cup olive oil

¼ teaspoon salt

¼ teaspoon white pepper

5 dashes Tabasco®

2 tablespoons fresh lime juice

Serves four to six

Combine all ingredients in a bowl and mix well. Cover and chill for at least 3 hours; then serve.

QUICK PARTY DIP

2 cups mayonnaise (see Index)

1 tablespoon onion, chopped

2 teaspoons dried tarragon

1½ teaspoons horseradish

1 teaspoon fresh parsley, chopped

½ teaspoon salt

½ teaspoon black pepper

Serves four to six

Combine all ingredients and mix thoroughly. Serve with celery, green peppers, asparagus, and broccoli.

REFRIED BEAN DIP

16 oz. canned refried beans

2 jalapeno peppers, finely chopped

½ cup sharp Cheddar cheese, grated

1 small onion, chopped

2 tablespoons picante sauce

Serves six

Mix all ingredients together in a saucepan and cook over a low heat until the cheese starts to melt. Serve immediately.

NEW MEXICO BEAN DIP

16 oz. canned refried beans

2 jalapeno peppers, finely chopped

1 cup sharp Cheddar cheese, grated

1 cup black olives, chopped

1 medium onion, finely chopped

1 garlic clove, minced

½ cup medium salsa

Serves six

Mix all ingredients together in a saucepan and cook over a low heat until the cheese starts to melt. Serve immediately.

HANNIBAL DIP

30 oz. canned garbanzo beans, rinsed and drained

3 garlic cloves, minced

¼ cup fresh lemon juice

3 tablespoons olive oil

1½ teaspoons salt

1 teaspoon ground cumin

3 dashes Tabasco®

Serves eight to ten

Combine all ingredients in a food processor until smooth. Serve with an acceptable cracker (see Brand Name Guide).

SCANDINAVIAN DIP

1 cup smoked salmon, chopped

4 oz. cream cheese, room temperature

½ cup heavy cream

½ cup sour cream

1 teaspoon fresh lemon juice

1½ teaspoons fresh dill, chopped

¼ teaspoon white pepper

Serves four to six

Combine all ingredients in a food processor until smooth. Place the dip in a serving bowl; cover, and refrigerate for 2 hours. Serve with celery, green peppers, asparagus, and broccoli or an acceptable cracker (see Brand Name Guide).

NORWEGIAN STUFFED EGGS

6 eggs, hard-boiled and peeled

⅓ cup smoked salmon, finely chopped

⅓ cup capers, finely chopped

¼ teaspoon salt

¼ teaspoon black pepper

½ cup mayonnaise (see Index)

2 tablespoons fresh parsley, minced

Serves six to eight

Halve the eggs lengthwise and carefully scoop out the yolks. In a bowl, mash the yolks with a fork and add the salmon, capers, salt, and pepper; fold in the mayonnaise. Fill the whites with the egg yolk mixture, and sprinkle the tops with parsley.

SARDINE STUFFED EGGS

8 eggs, hard-boiled and peeled

3½ oz. canned sardines, rinsed and drained

1 tablespoon fresh parsley, finely chopped

1 tablespoon fresh lemon juice

1 tablespoon Dijon mustard

4 dashes Tabasco®

4 tablespoons mayonnaise (see Index)

Paprika for garnish

Serves six to eight

Halve the eggs lengthwise and carefully scoop out the yolks. In a bowl, mash the yolks with a fork and add the sardines, parsley, lemon juice, mustard, and Tabasco.® Fold in the mayonnaise. Fill the egg whites with the egg yolk mixture, and sprinkle the tops with paprika.

STUFFED CURRIED EGGS

10 eggs, hard-boiled and peeled

1 tablespoon curry powder

2 teaspoons soy sauce

1 tablespoon dill relish

1 tablespoon fresh parsley, finely chopped

¼ teaspoon salt

¼ teaspoon black pepper

½ cup mayonnaise (see Index)

Paprika for garnish

Serves six to eight

Halve the eggs lengthwise and carefully scoop out the yolks. In a bowl, mash the yolks with a fork and add the curry powder, soy sauce, relish, parsley, salt, and pepper. Fold in the mayonnaise. Fill the whites with the egg yolk mixture, and sprinkle the tops with paprika.

GRECIAN STUFFED EGGS

12 eggs, hard-boiled and peeled

½ cup pitted black olives, chopped

1½ tablespoons horseradish

¼ teaspoon salt

¼ teaspoon black pepper

½ cup mayonnaise (see Index)

Paprika for garnish

Serves six to eight

Halve the eggs lengthwise and carefully scoop out the yolks. In a bowl, mash the yolks with a fork and add the black olives, horseradish, salt, and pepper. Fold in the mayonnaise. Fill the whites with the egg yolk mixture and sprinkle the tops with paprika.

LOUISIANA CRABMEAT SPREAD

1 lb. lump crabmeat

8 oz. cream cheese, room temperature

1 cup sharp Cheddar cheese, grated

2 green onions, finely chopped

6 tablespoons mayonnaise (see Index)

1 teaspoon Worcestershire sauce

1 tablespoon fresh lemon juice

⅛ teaspoon salt

4 teaspoons milk

4 dashes Tabasco®

Triscuit®

Preheat oven to 450° F.

Serves eight

In a bowl, combine the crabmeat, cream cheese, Cheddar cheese, green onion, mayonnaise, Worcestershire sauce, lemon juice, salt, milk, and Tabasco® very gently. Place a heaping teaspoon of the crabmeat mixture on Triscuit® and place in the oven for 6 to 8 minutes. Watch carefully and serve immediately.

CRAB AND EGG SALAD SPREAD

12 oz. lump crabmeat

4 hard-boiled eggs, peeled and chopped

½ cup mayonnaise (see Index)

½ cup sour cream

⅓ cup freshly grated Parmesan cheese

2 tablespoons Dijon mustard

¼ cup fresh dill, minced

2 green onions, finely chopped

1 tablespoon fresh lemon juice

Serves six to eight

Mix all ingredients together and chill. May be served with pumpernickel or cracker (see Brand Name Guide).

GORGONZOLA SPREAD

8 oz. cream cheese, room temperature

⅔ cup crumbled Gorgonzola cheese, room temperature

½ cup butter or margarine, room temperature

3 teaspoons milk

½ cup pimiento-stuffed olives, chopped

1 tablespoon fresh parsley, finely chopped

⅓ teaspoon garlic salt

Serves four

Mix all ingredients together and chill. Serve with an acceptable cracker (see Brand Name Guide).

CELERY AND STILTON SPREAD

½ cup Stilton cheese, room temperature

½ cup cream cheese, room temperature

3 tablespoons fresh celery, finely chopped

½ teaspoon black pepper

Serves four

Mix all ingredients together and chill. Serve with an acceptable cracker (see Brand Name Guide).

RED BEAN SPREAD

4 slices bacon

1 onion, finely chopped

1 garlic clove, minced

15 oz. canned red kidney beans, rinsed and drained

1 teaspoon black pepper

¼ cup water

1 cup sharp Cheddar cheese, grated

Preheat oven to 375° F.

Serves six

Cook bacon until crisp. Remove bacon and save drippings. Add onion and garlic to drippings and sauté until soft. Add beans and pepper; cook for 2 minutes. Add water and blend in a food processor. Remove from processor. Fold in crumbled bacon and cheese, reserving some cheese as a topper. Put into 2-cup baking dish. Top with remaining cheese and bake 10 to 15 minutes. May be served with pumpernickel or an acceptable cracker (see Brand Name Guide).

PISTACHIO SMOKED SALMON SPREAD

8 oz. cream cheese, room temperature

¼ lb. smoked salmon, finely chopped

2 tablespoons mayonnaise (see Index)

¾ cup pistachios, shelled and finely chopped

3 teaspoons fresh lemon juice

½ teaspoon Worcestershire sauce

Dash Tabasco®

Serves four

Mix all ingredients together and chill. May be served with pumpernickel or an acceptable cracker (see Brand Name Guide).

SARDINE SPREAD

3½ oz. canned sardines

8 oz. cream cheese, room temperature

4 green onions, finely chopped

1 bunch fresh parsley, stemmed and finely chopped

1 teaspoon lemon zest, finely grated

¼ teaspoon salt

¼ teaspoon white pepper

1 tablespoon fresh lemon juice

Serves four to six

Place all ingredients in a food processor until almost smooth. Pour into a bowl, cover, and chill for 3 hours. Serve with celery, green peppers, asparagus, and broccoli or an acceptable cracker (see Brand Name Guide).

TUNA ANCHOVY SPREAD

8 oz. cream cheese, room temperature

½ cup (1 stick) butter or margarine, softened

6½ oz. canned solid white tuna, drained

2 tablespoons mayonnaise (see Index)

1½ teaspoons anchovy paste

¼ teaspoon salt

¼ teaspoon white pepper

½ teaspoon Worcestershire sauce

4 dashes Tabasco®

Serves four to six

Mix all ingredients together and chill. May be served with pumpernickel, rye or an acceptable cracker (see Brand Name Guide).

STILTON SPREAD

6 oz. Stilton cheese, room temperature

4 oz. cream cheese, room temperature

2 tablespoons fresh lemon juice

2 teaspoons fresh chives, finely chopped

½ teaspoon paprika

2 tablespoons capers, finely chopped

Serves four

Mix all ingredients together and chill. Serve with celery, green peppers, asparagus, and broccoli or an acceptable cracker (see Brand Name Guide).

ROASTED EGGPLANT AND GARBANZO SPREAD

1 lb. eggplant, cubed

¼ cup olive oil

15½ oz. canned Garbanzo beans, drained and rinsed

¼ cup fresh parsley, finely chopped

¼ cup fresh mint leaves, finely chopped

4 garlic cloves, minced

1 large tomato, chopped

¼ cup capers

½ cup marinated artichoke hearts

¼ teaspoon salt

4 dashes Tabasco®

Preheat oven to 425° F

Serves six to eight

In a roasting pan, combine the eggplant and olive oil. Roast until tender, about 45 minutes. Transfer the eggplant to a food processor along with remaining ingredients and process until puréed. Serve immediately with acceptable crackers (see Brand Name Guide).

SMOKED SALMON PATÉ

1½ cups smoked salmon, chopped

8 oz. cream cheese, room temperature

¾ cup heavy cream

2 teaspoons lime juice

2½ teaspoons fresh dill, chopped

¼ teaspoon white pepper

Serves four to six

Mix all ingredients together and chill. May be served with pumpernickel or an acceptable cracker (see Brand Name Guide).

TOASTED SALTED ALMONDS

3 tablespoons melted butter or margarine, room temperature

3 tablespoons Worcestershire sauce

2 teaspoons salt

4 cups raw almonds

Preheat oven to 300° F.

Serves eight

Mix all the seasonings with the melted butter or margarine. Add the almonds and toss well. Spread on a large baking sheet and bake for 10 minutes. Remove to stir and toss the almonds with a spatula so they will bake evenly. Return to the oven for 10 minutes longer until the almonds have dried slightly. Let cool to room temperature and serve.

WALNUT ROQUEFORT SANDWICHES

½ cup Roquefort cheese, room temperature

½ cup butter or margarine, room temperature

24 walnut halves, shelled

Serves four

Blend the Roquefort cheese and the butter or margarine. Chill 30 minutes. Dab the mixture between 2 walnut halves. Press halves together. Serve immediately.

MEXICAN ALMONDS

⅓ cup butter or margarine, melted

1 tablespoon chili powder

2 teaspoons cumin

1 teaspoon salt

4 dashes Tabasco®

4 cups raw almonds

Preheat oven to 350° F.

Serves eight

Mix all the seasonings with the melted butter or margarine. Add the almonds and toss well. Spread on a large baking sheet and bake for 10 minutes. Remove to stir and toss the almonds with a spatula so they will bake evenly. Return to the oven for 10 minutes longer until the almonds have dried slightly. Let cool to room temperature and serve.

CHEDDAR CHEESE SPREAD

8 oz. sharp Cheddar cheese, grated

2 oz. butter or margarine, room temperature

2 tablespoons sherry

3 dashes Tabasco®

Serves eight

In a bowl, mix all ingredients together with a fork until well blended and creamy. Serve with celery sticks or acceptable crackers (see Brand Name Guide).

HAM AND CHEESE SPREAD

¾ cup cooked ham, finely chopped

1 cup sharp Cheddar cheese, grated

2 green onions, finely chopped

2 tablespoons capers

1 tablespoon Dijon mustard

¾ cup mayonnaise (see Index)

2 tablespoons sherry

salt and pepper to taste

Serves six to eight

In a bowl, mix all ingredients together with a fork until well blended and creamy. Serve with celery sticks or acceptable crackers (see Brand Name Guide).

CHEDDAR CHEESE AND GREEN ONION SPREAD

1 lb. sharp Cheddar cheese, room temperature and grated

4 tablespoons green onion, finely chopped

2 teaspoons Dijon mustard

2 tablespoons sherry

1 teaspoon Worcestershire sauce

3 dashes Tabasco®

Serves eight

In a bowl, mix all ingredients together with a fork until well blended and creamy. Serve with celery sticks or acceptable crackers (see Brand Name Guide).

ROAST BEEF HORSERADISH ROLLS

8 oz. cream cheese, room temperature

3 tablespoons horseradish

3 tablespoons chives, finely chopped

⅓ cup sour cream

¼ teaspoon salt

16 thin slices, rare roast beef

Serves ten to twelve

Blend all ingredients except roast beef. Lay roast beef slices on a platter and spread each slice with a layer of the mixture. Roll up each slice individually and secure with a toothpick. May be cut into smaller portions.

SALMON CREAM CHEESE ROLLS

3 oz. cream cheese, room temperature

2 tablespoons horseradish

¼ teaspoon black pepper

3 teaspoons capers, finely chopped

8 thin slices smoked salmon

Serves eight to ten

Blend all ingredients except smoked salmon. Lay salmon slices on a platter and spread each slice with a layer of the mixture. Roll up each slice individually and secure with a toothpick. May be cut into smaller portions.

TURKEY STILTON ROLLS

8 oz. Stilton cheese, room temperature

8 oz. cream cheese, room temperature

⅓ cup sour cream

1 garlic clove, minced

¼ teaspoon salt

¼ teaspoon black pepper

8 thin slices turkey breast

Serves ten to twelve

Blend all ingredients except turkey breast. Lay turkey slices on a platter and spread each slice with a layer of the mixture. Roll up each slice individually and secure with a toothpick. May be cut into smaller portions.

CAVIAR WITH AVOCADO

8 eggs, hard-boiled and peeled

2 small ripe avocados

4 romaine lettuce leaves

12 to 16 oz. black caviar

8 tablespoons parsley, finely chopped

2 lemons, halved and hollowed out

½ cup sour cream

8 tablespoons capers, finely chopped

8 tablespoons onion, finely chopped

Serves four

Separate the egg whites from the yolks. Finely chop the egg whites and set them aside. Repeat with the egg yolks, keeping them separate from the whites. Peel the avocados and split them in half lengthwise; remove the pits.

Place a romaine lettuce leaf on each of four salad plates. Center an avocado half, pit side up, on the lower half of each plate. Spoon 3 to 4 ounces of caviar into the pit of the avocados. On the upper portion of each plate, arrange in a crescent the following: ¼ of the chopped egg whites, 2 tablespoons parsley, a halved lemon filled with 2 tablespoons sour cream, 2 tablespoons capers, ¼ of the chopped egg yolks, and 2 tablespoons onion.

CAVIAR PIE

6 eggs, hard-boiled and peeled

½ cup (1 stick) butter or margarine, room temperature

¼ cup mayonnaise (see Index)

½ cup green onion, chopped

1 teaspoon fresh lemon juice

¼ teaspoon salt

¼ teaspoon white pepper

½ cup sour cream

2 oz. black caviar

Serves ten to twelve

In a food processor, blend until smooth all but the sour cream and caviar. Lightly grease a 3-cup mold with vegetable oil and fill with the mixture; chill overnight. Unmold and frost with sour cream; sprinkle with caviar. Serve with party rye or an acceptable cracker (see Brand Name Guide).

ENDIVE WITH CAVIAR

½ cup sour cream

3 tablespoons cream cheese, room temperature

3 endives, spears separated, rinsed, and dried

6 oz. black caviar

Serves ten to twelve

Mix the sour cream and the cream cheese until smooth. Spoon ½ teaspoon of the cheese mixture on the stem end of each endive spear. Top with ½ teaspoon of the caviar. Repeat with the remaining endive spears.

45

BUSTER CRAB PECAN

1 large egg
¼ cup milk
4 baby soft-shell crabs
Stone ground whole wheat flour for dredging
¼ cup (½ stick) plus 2 teaspoons butter or margarine
1 cup chopped pecans
1 tablespoon Worcestershire sauce
¾ cup creamy lemon butter sauce (see Index)
8 oz. lump crabmeat, picked over to remove any shell and cartilage
Salt and black pepper

Serves four

Clean the crabs by removing the eyes and gills; trim the tails. Sprinkle on both sides with salt and pepper.

Combine the egg and the milk in a shallow bowl and beat until well blended. Dredge the soft-shell crabs in flour, dip them in the egg wash, then redredge them in flour. Melt ¼ cup butter or margarine in a large sauté pan over medium heat. Add the crabs to the pan and cook until crisp, about 3 to 4 minutes over medium high heat, turning them once; the crabs are very delicate and should be handled gently during cooking. Remove the crabs from the pan and place them on heated serving plates.

Drain the sauté pan, leaving about 1 tablespoon of pan drippings. Add the pecans to the pan and sauté about 2 minutes. Reduce the heat to low and stir in the Worcestershire and lemon butter sauce. Remove the pan from direct heat until serving.

In a small skillet, melt 2 teaspoons of butter or margarine. Add the crabmeat and cook over medium heat for 1 to 2 minutes just until the crabmeat is warmed through; shake the pan or stir gently during cooking, being careful not to break apart the lumps of crabmeat. Top each soft-shell crab with 2 ounces (about ¼ cup) crabmeat, then drizzle with the pecan sauce.

BUSTER CRAB VINAIGRETTE

4 baby soft-shell crabs

¼ cup (½ stick) butter or margarine

Stone ground whole wheat flour for dusting

Salt and black pepper

½ cup warm vinaigrette dressing (see Index)

Serves four

Clean the crabs by removing the eyes and gills; trim the tails.

Melt the butter or margarine in a large sauté pan. Sprinkle the crabs on both sides with salt and pepper, then dust lightly with flour. Place the crabs in the pan and cook over moderately high heat for 3 minutes per side. The crabs are very delicate, so handle them gently during cooking. Place the cooked crabs on heated serving plates and top each with 2 tablespoons vinaigrette dressing.

SPICY CHICKEN WINGS

½ cup (1 stick) butter or margarine, melted

½ cup olive oil

3 tablespoons crushed red pepper

⅔ cup fresh lemon juice

5 garlic cloves, minced

3 teaspoons ground black pepper

6 lbs. chicken wings

Preheat oven to 425° F.

Serves ten to twelve

In a large bowl, combine all ingredients except the chicken wings and mix well. Rinse and pat dry the chicken wings. Cover with the sauce and toss to coat well. On baking sheets, place the wings and bake for 45 to 50 minutes, until golden brown.

ITALIAN WHITE BEANS WITH TUNA

1 garlic clove, minced

2 teaspoons fresh thyme, finely chopped

3 tablespoons red wine vinegar

¼ cup olive oil

1 teaspoon salt

¼ teaspoon black pepper

30 oz. canned Italian white beans, drained and rinsed

¾ cup red onion, chopped

13 oz. canned white tuna, packed in oil and drained

Serves eight to ten

In a large bowl, combine the garlic, thyme, vinegar, olive oil, salt, and pepper. Beat with a fork to blend. Add beans and red onion to bowl and toss to coat. Break tuna into chunks and toss lightly with bean mixture. Serve immediately.

BRIE BUTTER

1 lb. very ripe Brie

½ lb. butter or margarine, room temperature

½ cup dry white wine

Serves six to eight

Slice top and sides off Brie cheese. In a food processor, blend all ingredients together. Serve with acceptable crackers (see Brand Name Guide).

BAKED BRIE WITH PECANS

1 cup toasted pecans

8 inch wheel Brie

Preheat oven to 350° F.

Serves four to six

Toast pecans in oven for 12 to 14 minutes. Place wheel of Brie on baking dish and sprinkle with pecans. Bake in oven for 8 to 10 minutes. Serve with acceptable crackers (see Brand Name Guide).

BAKED MOZZARELLA, TOMATO AND PROSCIUTTO

8 slices Mozzarella cheese

8 slices tomato

1 teaspoon dried basil

8 thin slices prosciutto

½ cup dry white wine

4 tablespoons butter or margarine

Preheat oven to 425° F.

Serves four

On each slice of tomato, place a slice of Mozzarella cheese and sprinkle with basil. Cover each portion with prosciutto. Sprinkle with wine and dab with butter or margarine. Bake in oven for 6 to 10 minutes or until cheese begins to melt.

SAUCES

SPICY BARBECUE SAUCE

½ cup cooking oil
1 cup onion, finely chopped
½ cup green pepper, finely chopped
3 teaspoons garlic, finely chopped
2 tablespoons fresh parsley, finely chopped
1 cup beef broth or stock (see Index)
24 oz. canned tomato sauce
4 tablespoons red wine vinegar with garlic
2 tablespoons fresh lemon juice
¾ cup sugar free maple syrup
3 tablespoons Worcestershire sauce
1 teaspoon horseradish
2 teaspoons hot chili powder
2 teaspoons dry mustard
2 teaspoons salt
½ teaspoon cayenne pepper
6 dashes Tabasco®
3 tablespoons liquid smoke

Yields 4½ cups

Heat the cooking oil in a saucepan over moderate heat. Sauté the onion, green pepper, garlic, and parsley until soft. Add the remaining ingredients and cook for 20 to 30 minutes, stirring constantly. Use for barbecuing immediately or refrigerate.

MADEIRA ROQUEFORT SAUCE

2 oz. Roquefort cheese, crumbled
¼ cup Madeira wine
1 cup mayonnaise (see Index)
1 cup sour cream
2 garlic cloves, minced
2 green onions, chopped
¼ teaspoon salt
¼ teaspoon white pepper
3 dashes Tabasco®
½ teaspoon Worcestershire sauce
2 teaspoons lemon zest, finely grated

Yields 2½ cups

In a food processor, blend all ingredients until smooth.

Suggested use: Serve with chicken, steaks or roast beef

CAESAR SAUCE WITH STILTON

1 cup olive oil
2 tablespoons Stilton cheese, crumbled
2 teaspoons Dijon mustard
3 garlic cloves, minced
8 anchovy fillets, minced
2 teaspoons Worcestershire sauce
¾ cup freshly grated Parmesan cheese
1 tablespoon fresh lemon juice
¼ teaspoon salt
¼ teaspoon black pepper

Yields 2 cups

In a food processor, blend all ingredients until smooth.

Suggested use: Serve with fish, chicken, pork, lamb or beef

CAPER SAUCE

½ cup capers, drained and minced

2 cups olive oil

½ cup mayonnaise (see Index)

½ cup sour cream

¼ cup dry white wine

1 tablespoon fresh lemon juice

6 tablespoons fresh dill, minced

2 garlic cloves, minced

¼ teaspoon salt

¼ teaspoon white pepper

Yields 3½ cups

In a food processor, blend all ingredients except for the capers until smooth. Gently fold in the capers and serve or refrigerate.

Suggested use: Serve with seafood, chicken or lamb

CARPACCIO SAUCE

2 cups mayonnaise (see Index)

4 anchovy fillets, minced

3 teaspoons capers, drained and minced

2 bunches fresh parsley, chopped

4 teaspoons red wine vinegar

¼ teaspoon black pepper

3 dashes Tabasco®

Yields 2 cups

In a food processor, blend all ingredients, except for the capers, until smooth. Gently fold in the capers and serve or refrigerate.

Suggested use: Serve with grilled chicken, steaks or roast beef

CAVIAR SAUCE

4 oz. red caviar
1 cup sour cream
3 hard-boiled eggs, peeled and chopped
1 teaspoon lemon zest, finely grated
4 green onions, finely chopped
1 tablespoon fresh lemon juice

Yield 1½ cups

In a food processor, blend all ingredients except for 2 oz. of the caviar until smooth. Gently fold in the remaining 2 oz. of caviar and serve or refrigerate.

Suggested use: Serve with pasta, omelettes, poached or grilled salmon

COLD CUCUMBER SAUCE

1 large cucumber, peeled and chopped
1 small cucumber, peeled and chopped
2 cups sour cream
2 tablespoons capers, drained
½ cup green onion, chopped
2 tablespoons fresh dill, chopped
¼ teaspoon salt
¼ teaspoon white pepper
1 tablespoon fresh lemon juice

Yields 3 cups

In a food processor, blend all ingredients, except for the small cucumber, until smooth. Gently fold in the small cucumber, refrigerate, and serve.

Suggested use: Serve with seafood, chicken or lamb

CURRY SAUCE

½ cup mayonnaise (see Index)

½ cup sour cream

2 teaspoons curry powder

½ teaspoon ground ginger

¼ teaspoon cilantro, minced

1 tablespoon fresh lemon juice

Yields 1 cup

In a food processor, blend all ingredients until smooth.

Suggested use: Serve with seafood, chicken or lamb

DILL CREAM SAUCE

¼ cup fresh dill, minced

5 teaspoons red wine vinegar

1 hard-boiled egg yolk

2 teaspoons Dijon mustard

¾ cup sour cream

¼ teaspoon salt

¼ teaspoon white pepper

1 tablespoon lemon juice

Yields 2 cups

In a food processor, blend all ingredients until smooth.

Suggested use: Serve with seafood, chicken or lamb

DIJON MUSTARD SAUCE

2 cups mayonnaise (see Index)

4 tablespoons Dijon mustard

½ cup sour cream

1 tablespoon fresh lemon juice

Yields 2½ cups

In a food processor, blend all ingredients until smooth.

Suggested use: Serve with chicken, grilled steaks or roast beef

COLD MUSTARD MINT SAUCE

4 tablespoons Dijon mustard

3 tablespoons dry sherry

⅔ cup balsamic vinegar

2 tablespoons fresh mint, minced

Yields 1 cup

In a food processor, blend all ingredients until smooth.

Suggested use: Serve with chicken, pork, lamb or beef

57

LEMON TARRAGON SAUCE

1 cup mayonnaise (see Index)

1 cup sour cream

2 tablespoons lemon zest, finely grated

2 teaspoons Dijon mustard

½ teaspoon dried tarragon

1 green onion, chopped

¼ teaspoon salt

¼ teaspoon white pepper

1 tablespoon fresh lemon juice

Yields 2 cups

In a food processor, blend all ingredients until smooth.

Suggested use: Serve with seafood, chicken, veal or pork

CREAMY LEMON BUTTER SAUCE

½ cup beef broth or stock (see Index)

juice of 2 large lemons

2 cups (4 sticks) butter or margarine, room temperature

Yields 2 cups

In a medium-sized sauce pan, boil beef broth or stock, on high fire. Add the freshly squeezed lemon juice. Lower the fire and simmer until reduced by half. Add butter or margarine and whisk quickly. Remove pan from heat, whisking constantly, and return to heat, whisking constantly. Continue this process until all the butter or margarine is melted. Remove from heat and set aside. Serve immediately.

Suggested use: Serve with chicken, veal or seafood.

SMOKED SALMON SAUCE

8 oz. smoked salmon, minced

8 oz. cream cheese, room temperature

½ cup sour cream

⅓ cup mayonnaise (see Index)

2 tablespoons fresh dill, minced

¼ cup fresh parsley, minced

¼ cup onion, chopped

¼ cup green onion, finely chopped

¼ teaspoon salt

¼ teaspoon white pepper

1 tablespoon fresh lemon juice

2 dashes Tabasco®

Yields 3 cups

In a food processor, blend all ingredients until smooth.

Suggested use: Serve with pasta, omelettes, poached or grilled Salmon

CRABMEAT AND SHRIMP SAUCE

8 oz. lump crabmeat

8 oz. boiled shrimp, chopped

8 oz. cream cheese, room temperature

½ cup sour cream

½ cup mayonnaise (see Index)

2 tablespoons fresh dill, minced

3 teaspoons Dijon mustard

¼ cup fresh parsley, minced

¼ cup green onion, finely chopped

¼ teaspoon salt

¼ teaspoon white pepper

1 tablespoon fresh lemon juice

4 dashes Tabasco®

Yields 3 cups

In a food processor, blend all ingredients, except for 4 oz. of the crabmeat and 4 oz. of the shrimp, until smooth. Gently fold in the remaining crabmeat and shrimp; serve immediately or refrigerate.

Suggested use: Serve with fish, pasta or omelettes

SOUPS AND STOCKS

Soups

CREAM OF ASPARAGUS SOUP

½ cup onion, chopped

1 garlic clove, minced

½ cup (1 stick) butter or margarine

1½ lbs. fresh asparagus, peeled and cut into 1 inch pieces

2 cups chicken broth or stock (see Index)

¾ teaspoon basil

1 teaspoon salt

¼ teaspoon black pepper

2 dashes Tabasco®

1 tablespoon fresh lemon juice

1 cup half and half

Serves six

In a heavy pot, sauté onion and garlic in butter or margarine until soft. Add asparagus, chicken broth or stock, basil, salt, pepper, and Tabasco.® Simmer and cook about 20 minutes until asparagus are tender. Blend in a food processor until smooth. Reheat the mixture, add the lemon juice, and half and half, then serve.

ASPARAGUS AND SORREL SOUP

2 tablespoons olive oil

6 tablespoons butter or margarine

1 cup onion, chopped

2 lbs. asparagus, peeled and chopped

2 cups sorrel leaves, chopped

6 cups chicken broth or stock (see Index)

¼ teaspoon salt

¼ teaspoon white pepper

1 cup heavy cream

Serves six

Heat butter or margarine and olive oil in a heavy 8-quart pan. Sauté onion, stirring until softened, about 5 minutes. Add asparagus and sorrel; toss and stir another 3 to 4 minutes. Pour in chicken broth or stock, salt, and pepper. Simmer and cook about 20 minutes, until asparagus are tender. Cool slightly and purée in a food processor. Return to pan and gently whisk in heavy cream. Can be served warm or chilled.

CHILLED AVOCADO SOUP

3 ripe avocados, pitted and peeled

1 cup chicken broth or stock (see Index)

1 cup half and half

1 teaspoon salt

¼ teaspoon onion salt

1 teaspoon fresh lemon juice

Serves four

In a food processor, combine the avocados with the chicken broth or stock; process until smooth. Stir in the cream and seasonings. Pour into a glass container; cover and chill overnight. Just before serving the chilled soup add the fresh lemon juice.

AVOCADO AND DILL SOUP

2 large avocados, pitted and peeled
1 cup sour cream
2 cups fresh dill, finely chopped
2 cups cold chicken broth or stock (see Index)
1 teaspoon soy sauce
¼ teaspoon salt
¼ teaspoon white pepper

Serves four

In a food processor, mix all ingredients until smooth.
Chill for 20 minutes, then serve.

BROCCOLI VEGETABLE SOUP

4 slices bacon, chopped

4 cups fresh mushrooms, sliced

1 cup onion, chopped

1 tablespoon garlic, minced

1 tablespoon fresh parsley, minced

6 cups chicken broth or stock (see Index)

3 cups fresh broccoli, chopped

1 cup tomato, chopped

½ teaspoon thyme

½ teaspoon salt

¼ teaspoon white pepper

1 cup fresh spinach, chopped

3 tablespoons freshly grated Parmesan cheese

Serves six

In a heavy pot, sauté bacon until crisp. Add mushrooms, onion, garlic, and parsley. Cook for 5 minutes until soft. Add chicken broth or stock, broccoli, tomato, thyme, salt, and pepper. Cook on low heat for 30 minutes. Add spinach and cheese then cook for 5 additional minutes.

CREAM OF CELERY SOUP

6 tablespoons butter or margarine

16 stalks celery, chopped

1 tablespoon stone ground whole wheat flour

4 cups milk

1 teaspoon salt

1 teaspoon white pepper

2 cups half and half

Serves four

In a large saucepan, heat the butter or margarine and add the celery. Stir over a medium heat for 5 minutes. Sprinkle the flour over the celery, then add the milk, salt, and pepper. Bring to a boil, stirring constantly. Then simmer over a low heat for 20 minutes. In a food processor, purée the soup. Add the half and half, then reheat before serving.

CHILLED CUCUMBER SOUP

1 tablespoon olive oil

1 medium onion, chopped

2 garlic cloves, minced

2 large cucumbers, peeled and chopped

1½ cups milk

½ cup heavy cream

2 tablespoons fresh parsley, chopped

2 tablespoons fresh dill, chopped

½ teaspoon salt

½ teaspoon white pepper

Serves four

In a medium saucepan, heat the oil. Sauté the onion and garlic for 4 minutes. Add the cucumbers and sauté for 3 minutes. Stir in the milk, cream, parsley, dill, salt, and pepper. Cool and purée in a food processor until smooth; refrigerate and serve.

COLD CUCUMBER BISQUE

2 large cucumbers, peeled and chopped

1 medium onion, chopped

½ teaspoon salt

½ teaspoon white pepper

1 tablespoon Worcestershire sauce

3 dashes Tabasco®

2 cups chicken broth or stock (see Index)

2 cups sour cream

Serves four

In a food processor, blend the cucumbers, onion, salt, pepper, Worcestershire, and Tabasco® until smooth. Add the chicken broth or stock and sour cream. Blend well, chill and serve.

CREAM OF SWEET POTATO SOUP

1 tablespoon olive oil

1 medium onion, chopped

2 cups green onion, chopped

2 garlic cloves, minced

4 cups water

4 cups sweet potatoes, peeled and chopped

⅓ cup dry white wine

2 tablespoons fresh parsley, chopped

½ teaspoon salt

½ teaspoon white pepper

1 cup milk

Serves four

In a large saucepan, heat the oil and sauté the onion, green onion, and garlic until soft. Add the water, sweet potatoes, white wine, parsley, salt, pepper, and cook for 30 minutes, stirring occasionally. Let cool and blend in a food processor until smooth. Return the soup to the saucepan; stir in the milk, heat and serve.

STILTON SOUP

8 whole black peppercorns

3½ cups milk

1 large onion, chopped

1 bay leaf

6 tablespoons butter or margarine

3 tablespoons stone ground whole wheat flour

3 cups chicken broth or stock (see Index)

½ lb. Stilton cheese, crumbled

Serves four to six

In a saucepan, combine peppercorns, milk, onion, and bay leaf. Simmer for 15 minutes. Strain the milk mixture and set aside. In the saucepan, melt the butter or margarine and stir in the flour until smooth. Add the milk mixture and chicken broth or stock gradually. Bring to a boil; reduce heat and stir in Stilton until melted, then serve.

CREAM OF MUSHROOM AND ONION SOUP

½ cup (1 stick) butter or margarine
6 green onions, chopped
1 medium onion, chopped
1 teaspoon salt
1 teaspoon white pepper
5 cups chicken broth or stock (see Index)
1 lb. fresh mushrooms, thinly sliced
1¼ cups half and half

Serves six to eight

In a large saucepan, melt butter. Add onions, salt, pepper, and sauté for 10 minutes. Stir in the chicken broth or stock and bring to a boil. Cover and simmer for 10 minutes. Add half the mushrooms and purée in a food processor until smooth. Pour in the half and half, then heat. Add the remaining mushrooms and cook until tender.

TOMATO AND MUSHROOM SOUP

1 tablespoon butter or margarine

1 tablespoon olive oil

1 medium onion, thinly sliced

1 garlic clove, minced

1 cup tomato, chopped

4 cups fresh mushrooms, sliced

3 cups beef broth or stock (see Index)

¼ cup dry sherry

¼ cup tomato paste

¼ teaspoon white pepper

4 dashes Tabasco®

Serves four

In a medium saucepan, heat the butter or margarine with the olive oil; then sauté the onion and garlic about 5 minutes until soft. Add the tomato and mushrooms to the saucepan and cook 5 more minutes until tender. Stir in the beef broth or stock, sherry, tomato paste, white pepper, and Tabasco.® Bring to a boil; reduce the heat. Cover and simmer for 25 to 30 minutes.

CHILLED LIMA BEAN AND TOMATO SOUP

10 oz. frozen lima beans, cooked
2 cups tomatoes, chopped
½ cup green pepper, chopped
½ cup yellow pepper, chopped
1 cup cucumber, peeled and chopped
2 green onions, sliced
1 garlic clove, minced
1½ cups tomato juice
3 tablespoons red wine vinegar
1 tablespoon fresh dill, chopped
¼ teaspoon salt
6 dashes Tabasco®

Serves four

In a large mixing bowl, combine lima beans, tomatoes, green pepper, yellow pepper, cucumber, onion, and garlic. Stir in the tomato juice, vinegar, dill, salt, and Tabasco.® Refrigerate for at least 2 hours, then serve.

VEGETABLE GUMBO

2 tablespoons olive oil

1 medium onion, finely chopped

1 red bell pepper, chopped

1 small zucchini, chopped

3 stalks celery, sliced

3 garlic cloves, minced

6 cups vegetable stock (see Index)

14 oz canned tomatoes, mashed

½ cup brown rice

2 teaspoons dried oregano

1½ teaspoons dried thyme

1 teaspoon salt

¼ teaspoon ground black pepper

¼ teaspoon cayenne pepper

¼ cup fresh parsley, chopped

15 oz. canned red kidney beans, drained

4 dashes Tabasco®

Serves eight

In a large saucepan, heat the oil and cook the onion, red bell pepper, zucchini, celery, and garlic over medium heat until soft. Stir in the vegetable stock, tomatoes, rice, and dried seasonings; cook over low heat for an hour. Stir in the parsley, beans, Tabasco,® and cook for an additional 10 minutes. Let gumbo stand for 30 minutes before serving.

GARBANZO BEAN SOUP

1 tablespoon butter or margarine

2 cups fresh mushrooms, sliced

½ cup onion, chopped

2 garlic cloves, minced

30 oz. beef broth or stock (see Index)

½ cup small whole grain pasta shells

16 oz. canned tomatoes, chopped

15 oz. canned garbanzo beans, drained

¼ cup fresh basil, finely chopped

1 tablespoon fresh thyme, finely chopped

Serves four

In a large saucepan, heat the butter or margarine and cook the mushrooms, onion, and garlic until soft. Add the beef broth or stock. Bring to a boil and stir in the pasta. Return to a boil and cook until pasta is tender. Add tomatoes and garbanzo beans. Before serving, stir in the fresh basil and thyme.

RED BEAN GUMBO

1 lb. red kidney beans, dried
10 cups cold water
1 cup onion, chopped
1 cup celery, chopped
1 cup green pepper, chopped
1 tablespoon garlic, minced
6 strips of bacon, chopped
1½ cups tasso (see note below), chopped
1 tablespoon thyme leaves
1 tablespoon filé powder
32 shucked oysters
1 lb. medium shrimp, peeled and deveined
1 lb. lump crabmeat, picked over to remove any shell and cartilage
Salt and black pepper
4 cups cooked brown rice (see Index)

Serves eight

Place the beans in a stockpot and add 10 cups cold water. Bring the beans to a boil over high heat, then reduce the heat to medium and cook for 10 minutes. Add the onion, celery, bell pepper, garlic, bacon, tasso, thyme, and filé. Cook the mixture, loosely covered, at a low boil about 1½ hours until the beans begin to break apart; stir frequently. Purée two-thirds of the bean mixture in a food processor or mash through a fine sieve. Pour the bean purée into a large pot and add the oysters, shrimp, and remaining third of the cooked beans. Simmer the soup for 5 minutes, then stir in the crabmeat. Season the gumbo with salt and pepper to taste, then serve over warm cooked brown rice.

Note: Tasso is highly-seasoned Cajun smoked ham. If unavailable,
substitute smoked ham and add cayenne pepper to taste.

OYSTERS ROCKEFELLER SOUP

2 cups (about 48) shucked oysters
2 quarts cold water
¾ cup (1½ sticks) butter or margarine
¾ cup celery, chopped
½ cup stone ground whole wheat flour
⅓ cup Herbsaint or Pernod
8 oz. fresh spinach leaves, washed, stemmed, and coarsely chopped
¼ cup fresh parsley, finely chopped
2 cups heavy cream
Salt and white pepper

Serves eight to ten

Place the oysters in a large saucepan and cover with 2 quarts of cold water. Cook over medium heat just until the oysters begin to curl, about 5 minutes. Strain the oysters, reserving the stock and set them aside.

Melt the butter in a large pot and sauté the celery until tender. Stir in the flour, then add the oysters and oyster stock. Reduce the heat and simmer for 10 minutes until thickened. Add the Herbsaint, spinach, and parsley; season to taste with salt and pepper. Pour in the cream and simmer several minutes until the soup is hot, then serve.

CRAB BISQUE

10 lbs. (about 20 crabs) live hard-shell crabs, preferably female
1 lb. (4 sticks) butter or margarine
1 jumbo onion, coarsely chopped
4 celery stalks, coarsely chopped
8 medium tomatoes, quartered
1½ cups parsley, chopped
12 garlic cloves, minced
6 bay leaves
12 oz. (1½ cups) tomato paste
2 tablespoons thyme leaves
2 gallons cold water
3 oz. bag of crab boil
1 cup dry white wine
8 heaping tablespoons paprika
¼ teaspoon cayenne pepper
1½ tablespoons saffron
1¼ cups stone ground whole wheat flour
1 teaspoon salt
½ cup brandy
2 cups heavy cream
3 lbs. lump crabmeat, picked over to remove any shell and cartilage
Preheat oven to 375° F.

Serves ten

Clean the crabs by soaking them in tap water about 1 hour. In a 12-quart oven-proof roasting pan, melt 1 cup of the butter or margarine then add the onion, celery, tomatoes, parsley, garlic, bay leaves, tomato paste, and thyme. Stir the mixture together over moderately high heat and cook until hot, about 10 minutes.

Cover the crabs with a clean towel and, using a mallet, kill and crack the crabs into large pieces. Add the cracked crabs to the roasting pan and cook on top of the stove for 5 minutes, then transfer to the hot oven and roast for 25 minutes, stirring occasionally, until the crabs turn red.

While the crabs are roasting, combine 2 gallons of cold water, the crab boil, wine, paprika, and cayenne in a 24-quart stockpot. Bring the mixture to a boil, then add the contents of the roasting pan. Stir in the saffron and cook for 2 to 3 hours over medium-high heat until reduced to about 1 gallon of stock.

Strain the reduced stock into another large pot and discard the crab pieces and vegetables. Let the stock sit undisturbed for 20 minutes, then strain it through a fine sieve. Next, line the strainer with a single layer of cheesecloth and strain the stock again; repeat this step, then double the thickness of the cheesecloth and strain once more. Strain one final time through a double layer of cheesecloth and let the stock settle for another 20 minutes.

Melt the remaining cup of butter or margarine in a medium skillet and blend in the flour. Whisk the mixture over medium heat for 2 to 3 minutes.

Warm the stock over medium heat, then incorporate 6 to 8 tablespoons of the roux into the liquid, whisking until thickened. Stir in the salt, brandy, cream, and crabmeat. Cook the soup until smooth and hot, then serve.

CREAM OF CRAB SOUP

¼ cup (½ stick) butter

1½ cups onion, finely chopped

2 tablespoons stone ground whole wheat flour

1½ quarts (6 cups) heavy cream

1 lb. lump crabmeat, picked over to remove any shell and cartilage

2 tablespoons fresh parsley, chopped

Salt and white pepper

Serves eight

Melt the butter or margarine in a large saucepan or Dutch oven and sauté the onion until clear and tender. Blend in the flour; cook the mixture for 5 minutes, stirring frequently. Pour in the cream and season with salt and pepper to taste. Cook over medium heat, about 20 minutes, stirring occasionally. Add the crabmeat and parsley; cook an additional 5 minutes, then serve.

REDFISH SOUP

2 medium onions, chopped

6 stalks celery, chopped

4 garlic cloves, minced

4 tablespoons butter or margarine

1 cup fresh parsley, chopped

32 oz. canned tomatoes

1 cup dry white wine

6 bay leaves

2 green peppers, chopped

2 teaspoons basil

2 teaspoons oregano

4 teaspoons Dijon mustard

1 tablespoon horseradish

1 cup tomato juice

1 cup water

½ teaspoon salt

½ teaspoon white pepper

¼ teaspoon cayenne pepper

4 dashes Tabasco®

3 lbs. Redfish fillets or any white fish of your choice, cut into 1 inch pieces

Serves six

   In a Dutch oven, sauté the onion, celery, and garlic in butter or margarine. Add the remaining ingredients, except for the fish. Cover and simmer for 30 minutes. Add the Redfish and simmer for an additional 15 minutes, then serve.

Stocks

CHICKEN STOCK

3 lbs. chicken bones and parts	
1 small onion, chopped	
1 celery stalk, chopped	
1 garlic clove	
3 quarts cold water	

Yields 1½ quarts

Combine all the ingredients in a stockpot and cover with 3 quarts cold water. Bring the stock to a boil over high heat, skimming away the residue that rises to the surface. Reduce the heat and cook at a low rolling boil until reduced by half, about 2 hours. Strain the stock and use immediately or cover and refrigerate. Chicken stock can be frozen in smaller quantities for use in a variety of recipes.

BEEF STOCK

1 lb. beef bones
1 small white onion, chopped
1 celery stalk, chopped
1 garlic clove
½ bunch scallions, chopped
4 quarts cold water
Preheat oven to 450° F.

Yields 2 quarts

Arrange the beef bones in a single layer in a roasting pan. Roast in a hot oven until brown, about 15 minutes, stirring the bones occasionally.

Transfer the bones to a stockpot and add the remaining ingredients; cover with 4 quarts cold water. Bring the stock to a boil over high heat, skimming away the residue from the surface. Lower the heat and cook at a low rolling boil until reduced by half, about 2 hours. Strain and use immediately or freeze in smaller portions for use in a variety of recipes.

VEGETABLE STOCK

¾ lb. mixed vegetables and trimmings, chopped celery, leeks, scallions, parsley

2½ quarts water

1 onion, chopped

2 bay leaves, torn

salt and pepper to taste

Yields 2 quarts

Put all ingredients in a large pot. Add water and bring to a boil. Simmer, uncovered, for 1 hour, then drain.

FISH STOCK

1½ quarts cold water

1 lb. fish bones and trimmings

½ of a lemon

½ cup dry white wine

Yields 3 cups

Bring 1½ quarts of cold water to a boil in a large saucepan, along with the lemon and white wine. When the water reaches a rolling boil, add the fish bones and trimmings. Lower the heat and simmer until reduced by half, about 2 hours. Drain and refrigerate, covered, for several days or freeze for future use.

SHRIMP STOCK

Shells and tails from 4 lbs. shrimp
8 cups water
2 cups dry white wine
3 bay leaves
6 garlic cloves
8 green onions, chopped
1 cup fresh parsley, coarsely chopped
4 stalks celery, chopped
1 teaspoon salt
1 teaspoon white pepper

Yields 2 quarts

Place all ingredients in a large pot; add the water and bring to a boil. Leave uncovered and simmer for an hour. Strain the stock and use immediately or cover and refrigerate.

SALADS,
SALAD DRESSINGS
AND
MAYONNAISES

STEAMED ARTICHOKES

4 medium artichokes

2 lemons, halved

¼ cup celery, chopped

4 garlic cloves

pinch of salt

pinch of black pepper

6 tablespoons olive oil

1 teaspoon garlic powder

½ teaspoon white pepper

¾ teaspoon salt

½ teaspoon black pepper

salad dressing or mayonnaise (see Index)

Serves four

Wash the artichokes, then remove the stems and trim the sharp points from the leaves. Fill a large pot ¾ full with cold water. To the water, add the lemons, celery, garlic cloves, the pinches of salt and black pepper, and 3 tablespoons of the olive oil. Bring the water to a boil, then stand the artichokes upright in the pan. Sprinkle the artichokes with the garlic powder, white pepper, salt, and black pepper. Then drizzle the artichokes with the remaining 3 tablespoons of olive oil. Place a plate or other weight on top of the artichokes to keep them in position during cooking. Cook the artichokes at a rolling boil until tender, about 50 minutes. Remove the artichokes from the water, drain them, and let cool. Serve artichokes hot or cold with choice of salad dressing or mayonnaise for dipping.

EGG SALAD WITH ASPARAGUS AND DILL DRESSING

8 oz. cooked fresh asparagus, chopped

8 hard-boiled eggs, peeled and chopped

2 green onions, finely chopped

2 tablespoons pimiento, chopped

Serves four

Dressing:

¼ cup mayonnaise (see Index)

1 teaspoon fresh dill, minced

1 teaspoon Dijon mustard

½ teaspoon white wine vinegar

¼ teaspoon salt

⅛ teaspoon black pepper

In a mixing bowl, combine the asparagus, eggs, green onions, and pimiento. In a small mixing bowl, stir together the mayonnaise, dill, mustard, vinegar, salt, and pepper. Toss the dressing with the asparagus and egg mixture.

AVOCADOS WITH GORGONZOLA DRESSING

2 ripe avocados

2 tablespoons red onion, finely chopped

⅓ cup Gorgonzola cheese, crumbled

2 tablespoons balsamic vinegar

½ teaspoon salt

¼ teaspoon black pepper

3 tablespoons olive oil

Serves four

Cut each avocado in half and remove pit. In a small bowl, combine the red onion, Gorgonzola, vinegar, salt, pepper, and olive oil. Stir to mix. Cover each avocado hollow with the dressing and enjoy!

BROCCOLI AND CELERY SALAD

3 cups broccoli florets

¾ cup celery, chopped

¼ cup onion, finely chopped

⅓ cup sharp Cheddar cheese, grated

¼ cup mayonnaise (see Index)

¼ cup sour cream

2 tablespoons Dijon mustard

½ teaspoon salt

¼ teaspoon black pepper

Serves four

In a bowl, combine all ingredients and toss vigorously. Cover and refrigerate for 2 hours, then serve.

BRUSSEL SPROUTS WITH DILL DRESSING

10 oz. cooked brussels sprouts
¼ cup olive oil
1 tablespoon fresh lemon juice
½ cup red onion, thinly sliced
½ teaspoon fresh dill, minced
½ teaspoon garlic powder
½ teaspoon salt
¼ teaspoon black pepper

Serves four

In a glass bowl, combine all ingredients and toss vigorously. Cover and refrigerate for 2 hours, then serve.

CUCUMBER AND RADISH SALAD

2 cups cucumbers, peeled and thinly sliced
1½ cups radishes, thinly sliced
1 cup sour cream
2 tablespoons fresh dill, minced
½ teaspoon salt
¼ teaspoon white pepper

Serves four

In a bowl, combine all ingredients and toss vigorously. Cover and refrigerate for 2 hours, then serve.

GARBANZO BEAN SALAD

2 cups cucumbers, peeled and chopped
1½ cups green pepper, cored and chopped
1½ cups tomato, chopped
¼ cup onion, chopped
½ cup pitted black olives, drained and sliced
15 oz. canned garbanzo beans, rinsed and drained

Serves six to eight

Dressing:

⅓ cup olive oil
3 tablespoons fresh lemon juice
½ teaspoon white pepper
1½ teaspoons salt
4 teaspoons white vinegar

In a large bowl, combine all ingredients and mix well. Cover and refrigerate overnight, then serve.

GREEN BEANS AND FETA SALAD

1½ lbs. cooked green beans

¾ cup red onion, chopped

4 oz. Feta cheese, crumbled

Serves four

Dressing:

8 oz. sour cream

¼ teaspoon salt

¼ teaspoon black pepper

1 teaspoon fresh mint, minced

1½ tablespoons olive oil

2 tablespoons white wine vinegar

In a bowl, combine all ingredients and toss vigorously. Cover and refrigerate for 2 hours, then serve.

GREEN BEANS AND TOMATO SALAD

1½ lbs. cooked green beans

4 medium tomatoes, chopped

1 cup onion, chopped

4 tablespoons olive oil

3 tablespoons fresh lemon juice

3 garlic cloves, minced

¾ teaspoon salt

4 dashes Tabasco®

Serves four

In a bowl, combine all ingredients and toss vigorously. Cover and refrigerate overnight, then serve.

ATHENS SALAD

1 head iceberg lettuce, chopped

1½ cups cucumber, peeled and chopped

1¼ cups Feta cheese, crumbled

2 tomatoes, quartered

6 oz. pitted large black olives, drained and chopped

¾ cup olive oil

⅓ cup red wine vinegar

1 tablespoon dried oregano

1 teaspoon garlic powder

½ teaspoon salt

½ teaspoon black pepper

Serves four

In a bowl, combine all ingredients; toss well and serve.

GREEK TOMATO SALAD

1 garlic clove, minced

3 large tomatoes, chopped

12 pitted black olives, halved

1 cup Feta cheese, crumbled

3 tablespoons red wine vinegar

½ cup olive oil

½ teaspoon dried oregano

½ teaspoon dried thyme

¼ teaspoon salt

¼ teaspoon black pepper

Serves four

In a bowl, toss all ingredients together well. Cover and refrigerate for at least 4 hours, then serve.

ITALIAN TOMATO SALAD

4 cups tomato, coarsely chopped

1 lb. Mozzarella cheese, diced

Serves four

Dressing:

½ cup olive oil

¼ cup balsamic vinegar

½ teaspoon dried basil

½ teaspoon salt

½ teaspoon black pepper

In a bowl, toss all ingredients together well. Cover and refrigerate for at least 4 hours, then serve.

VEGETABLE SALAD

2 red bell peppers, cored and chopped

2 green bell peppers, cored and chopped

½ lb. fresh mushrooms, sliced

½ cup pimiento-stuffed olives

1 head cauliflower, coarsely chopped

1 cup pitted black olives

Serves four to six

Dressing:

½ cup red wine vinegar

½ cup olive oil

2 tablespoons onion, chopped

2 tablespoons fresh parsley, chopped

½ teaspoon garlic, minced

½ teaspoon salt

¼ teaspoon black pepper

4 dashes Tabasco®

In a bowl, toss ingredients together well. Cover and refrigerate for 2 hours, then serve.

LAYERED MEXICAN SALAD

15 oz. canned black beans, rinsed and drained

4 cups shredded iceberg lettuce

1 medium tomato, chopped

1½ cups sharp Cheddar cheese, shredded

¼ cup pitted black olives, sliced

¼ cup green onion, chopped

1 recipe of the Fresh Avocado Dip (see Index)

1 cup tomato, chopped for garnish

Serves four to six

In a large glass bowl, layer black beans, lettuce, tomato, cheese, olives, and onion. Spread avocado dip over the top of the salad. Sprinkle with chopped tomato. Cover and refrigerate for 2 hours. Before serving, toss salad together.

SPICY GAZPACHO SALAD

1 large cucumber, peeled and sliced into quarters

1 green pepper, cored and cut into strips

1 yellow pepper, cored and cut into strips

3 medium tomatoes, coarsely chopped

1 large avocado, peeled and coarsely chopped

1½ cups sharp Cheddar cheese, grated

½ cup pitted black olives, drained and sliced

Serves four

Dressing:

½ cup olive oil

2 tablespoons fresh lime juice

1 large garlic clove, minced

1 tablespoon onion, finely chopped

2 teaspoons fresh cilantro, finely chopped

¾ teaspoon salt

¼ teaspoon cayenne pepper

¼ teaspoon cumin

2 jalapeno peppers, minced

½ teaspoon black pepper

In a bowl, combine all the ingredients. Toss well with the dressing, then serve.

BLACK BEAN SALAD

15 oz. canned black beans, rinsed and drained
8 cups shredded iceberg lettuce
1 cup red bell pepper, chopped
½ cup onion, chopped
⅓ cup olive oil
2 tablespoons fresh lemon juice
1 teaspoon garlic powder
2 tablespoons fresh parsley, finely chopped
¼ teaspoon salt
¼ teaspoon black pepper
2 dashes Tabasco®

Serves four to six

In a bowl, combine all the ingredients and toss well. Cover and refrigerate for 2 hours, then serve.

HERBED RED BEAN SALAD

2 cups canned red kidney beans, rinsed and drained

½ cup red wine vinegar

8 tablespoons olive oil

4 garlic cloves, minced

1 tablespoon fresh mint, minced

1 tablespoon fresh basil, minced

1 teaspoon fresh thyme, minced

1 teaspoon fresh rosemary, minced

1 teaspoon fresh oregano, minced

¼ teaspoon salt

¼ teaspoon black pepper

¼ cup pitted black olives, chopped

¼ cup pitted green olives, chopped

½ cup green onion, chopped

Serves six

In a bowl, combine all the ingredients and toss well. Cover and refrigerate for 2 hours, then serve.

WHITE BEAN SALAD

2 cups canned white beans, rinsed and drained
2 tablespoons fresh lemon juice
⅓ cup olive oil
1 garlic clove, minced
2 tablespoons fresh parsley, finely chopped
¼ teaspoon salt
¼ teaspoon black pepper

Serves four to six

In a bowl, combine all the ingredients and toss well. Cover and refrigerate for 2 hours, then serve.

LENTIL SALAD

1 lb. lentils, cooked
1 large bunch parsley, finely chopped
1 bunch green onions, chopped
8 medium tomatoes, chopped
1 large garlic clove, minced
¼ teaspoon salt
¼ teaspoon black pepper
½ cup olive oil
1 cup fresh lemon juice

Serves four

In a bowl, combine all the ingredients and toss well. Cover and refrigerate for 2 hours, then serve.

GARLIC SALAD

| 2 large garlic cloves, minced |
| 1/2 teaspoon salt |
| 1/2 teaspoon black pepper |
| 2 teaspoons Dijon mustard |
| 2 tablespoons fresh lemon juice |
| 2/3 cup olive oil |
| 3 tablespoons freshly grated Parmesan cheese |
| 2 cups iceberg lettuce, cut into bite-size pieces |
| 2 cups romaine lettuce, cut into bite-size pieces |

Serves four

In a salad bowl, mash together the garlic, salt, pepper, and mustard. Stir in lemon juice, oil, cheese, and mix well. Toss thoroughly with lettuce and serve.

MAUDE'S TABLE SIDE SALAD

1 head iceberg lettuce
1 cup hearts of palm, sliced
2 hard-boiled eggs, peeled and chopped
¾ cup cooked bacon, crumbled
¼ cup green onion, chopped
¾ cup Blue cheese, crumbled
½ teaspoon Worcestershire sauce
½ teaspoon salt
½ teaspoon black pepper
¼ cup red wine vinegar
½ cup vegetable oil
Cherry tomatoes for garnish

Serves four

Core the iceberg lettuce and wash the leaves. Reserve 4 large leaves and chop the remaining lettuce into bite-size pieces. Place the chopped lettuce in a large bowl. Add the remaining ingredients, except the vinegar and oil. Pour the vinegar and oil over the salad and toss until the ingredients are well coated.

Place lettuce leaves on four chilled plates. Mound salad in the center of each plate and garnish with cherry tomatoes.

REX SALAD

2 heads iceberg lettuce

4 hard-boiled eggs, peeled and chopped

1 cup green onion, chopped

1 cup cooked bacon, crumbled

1 cup Blue cheese, crumbled

28 oz. canned artichoke hearts, drained and quartered

14 oz. canned hearts of palm, drained and sliced

¾ cup Classical French dressing (see Index)

1¼ cups Roquefort dressing (see Index)

Serves eight

Wash and core the lettuce. Reserve 4 large leaves for presentation; chop the remaining lettuce into bite-size pieces.

Place the chopped lettuce into a large bowl with the eggs, chives, bacon, Blue cheese, artichoke hearts, and hearts of palm. Toss the ingredients, then add the French and Roquefort dressings. Toss the salad until well coated with dressing, then mound on chilled plates lined with lettuce leaves.

HOT BEEF SALAD

6 cups romaine lettuce, chopped
3 teaspoons olive oil
1 medium green pepper, chopped
¾ lb. beef flank steak, cut into thin strips
½ cup Italian dressing (see Index)
1 tablespoon freshly grated Parmesan cheese
1 tablespoon ground black pepper

Serves four

Divide the romaine lettuce among 4 salad plates. In a large skillet, heat 2 teaspoons of the oil and cook the green pepper for 1 to 2 minutes. Add the remaining teaspoon of oil, the beef, and cook for 2 to 3 minutes. Pour the salad dressing over the beef and cook until heated. Spoon the beef mixture over the lettuce. Sprinkle with the cheese and pepper. Serve immediately.

ROAST BEEF POOR BOY SALAD

2 heads romaine lettuce, chopped

1½ lbs. medium-rare roast beef, chopped

1½ cups red onion, sliced

3 medium tomatoes, chopped

Serves eight

Dressing:

1½ cups mayonnaise (see Index)

¾ cup sour cream

4 tablespoons horseradish

2 tablespoons Dijon mustard

½ teaspoon black pepper

½ teaspoon salt

4 tablespoons olive oil

In a small bowl, combine the dressing ingredients and set aside. In a large bowl, mix the remaining ingredients. Pour the dressing over the salad and toss well. Serve immediately.

NEW YORK DELI SALAD

6 cups shredded cabbage

3 cups lean corned beef, cooked and chopped

1½ cups shredded Swiss cheese

12 oz. Thousand Island dressing (see Index)

Serves six to eight

In a large bowl, combine all the ingredients, except the dressing. Cover and chill until ready to use. Just before serving, pour dressing over ingredients and toss.

FRENCH CHICKEN SALAD

3 cups chicken breast, cooked and chopped
¾ cup mayonnaise (see Index)
2 tablespoons Dijon mustard
1 tablespoon fresh lemon juice
3 garlic cloves, minced
½ cup red bell pepper, chopped
½ cup green onion, chopped
4 cups shredded lettuce

Serves four

In a large bowl, combine all ingredients and mix well, except for lettuce. Divide the lettuce among 4 salad plates and top each bed of lettuce with the chicken salad.

TURKEY SALAD VINAIGRETTE

3 cups cooked turkey breast, chopped
1 head romaine lettuce, chopped
8 oz. fresh spinach, chopped
3 green onions, chopped
1 cup pecans, chopped

Serves four

Dressing:

1½ cups olive oil
⅓ cup red wine vinegar
2 tablespoons Dijon mustard
2 garlic cloves, minced
6 tablespoons mayonnaise (see Index)

In a large bowl, combine all the ingredients except the dressing. Cover and chill until ready to use. Blend dressing; pour over turkey mixture and toss well.

TURKEY AND WILD RICE SALAD

4 cups cooked wild rice

2 cups turkey breast, cooked and chopped

2 cups tomato, chopped

½ cup green pepper, chopped

¾ cup green onion, chopped

⅓ cup fresh parsley, chopped

⅓ cup balsamic vinegar

2 tablespoons olive oil

2 teaspoons garlic cloves, minced

Serves six

In a large bowl, combine the wild rice, turkey, tomato, green pepper, green onion, and parsley. In another small bowl, combine the vinegar, oil, and garlic, mixing well. Pour over the turkey mixture and toss.

WILD RICE SALAD

4 cups cooked wild rice

4 tablespoons olive oil

2 tablespoons red wine vinegar

2 tablespoons Dijon mustard

1 teaspoon ground black pepper

salt to taste

½ cup green onion, chopped

½ cup toasted pecans, chopped

1 tablespoon fresh lemon juice

Serves four

In a large bowl, toss wild rice with olive oil, vinegar, mustard, pepper, salt, green onion, and pecans. Let stand at room temperature for 2 hours. Just before serving, add lemon juice and toss.

CHEESY PASTA SALAD

1 lb. cooked whole grain pasta shells

1 cup ham, cooked and chopped

3 cups mayonnaise (see Index)

½ cup freshly grated Parmesan cheese

½ cup red wine vinegar

1 teaspoon oregano

1 teaspoon thyme

½ teaspoon salt

½ teaspoon black pepper

1 teaspoon garlic powder

6 hard-boiled eggs, peeled and chopped

2 cups Mozzarella cheese, diced

1 red bell pepper, chopped

6 green onions, finely chopped

Serves four to six

In a large bowl, mix all ingredients. Cover and refrigerate for 3 hours, then serve.

SHRIMP AND PASTA SALAD

1 lb. cooked shrimp, peeled, deveined, and chopped

1 lb. cooked whole grain elbow macaroni

1 cup olive oil

¾ cup fresh lemon juice

1 cup fresh basil leaves

2 garlic cloves, minced

1 teaspoon ground black pepper

¾ cup freshly grated Parmesan cheese

Serves six to eight

In a food processor, combine the olive oil, lemon juice, basil leaves, garlic, pepper, and cheese. Toss with the shrimp and pasta. Serve immediately.

CRABMEAT AND CHEDDAR CHEESE SALAD

1 lb. lump crabmeat

½ cup sharp Cheddar cheese, grated

½ cup pitted green olives, chopped

2 green onions, finely chopped

2 stalks celery, finely chopped

4 tablespoons mayonnaise (see Index)

2 tablespoons Dijon mustard

2 tablespoons red wine vinegar

salt and pepper to taste

Serves four

In a bowl, combine all ingredients. Cover and refrigerate for 2 hours, then serve.

Salad Dressings

CLASSICAL FRENCH

| 2½ cups olive oil |
| 1 cup red wine vinegar |
| 1½ oz. Worcestershire sauce |
| 1 teaspoon Tabasco® |
| 1¼ tablespoons black pepper |
| ¾ tablespoon salt |
| ¾ teaspoon Dijon mustard |
| 4 large garlic pods, minced |
| juice of one medium lemon |

Yields 4 cups

Blend all ingredients in a food processor. Shake well before each use.

GARLIC DRESSING

| 2½ cups olive oil |
| 5 garlic cloves, minced |
| 2 tablespoons Dijon mustard |
| 8 tablespoons tarragon vinegar |
| 6 tablespoons fresh lemon juice |
| 1 teaspoon salt |
| 2 teaspoons black pepper |

Yields 3½ cups

Blend all ingredients in a food processor until smooth.

ITALIAN DRESSING

¾ cup olive oil

¼ cup fresh lemon juice

2 tablespoons anchovy paste

2 tablespoons green onion, chopped

3 garlic cloves, minced

1 teaspoon Dijon mustard

2 tablespoons freshly grated Parmesan cheese

½ teaspoon black pepper

Yields 1 cup

In a bowl, use a hand mixer or whisk to blend ingredients until smooth.

QUICK CAESAR SALAD DRESSING

2 garlic cloves, minced

⅔ cup olive oil

2 tablespoons red wine vinegar

1 tablespoon fresh lemon juice

1 teaspoon Worcestershire sauce

2 dashes Tabasco®

2 raw egg yolks

2 oz. anchovy fillets

2 tablespoons freshly grated Parmesan cheese

½ teaspoon black pepper

Yields 1 cup

Blend all ingredients in a food processor until smooth.

DIJON PARMESAN DRESSING

⅓ cup olive oil

3 tablespoons Dijon mustard

2 tablespoons tarragon vinegar

1 tablespoon fresh lemon juice

⅓ cup freshly grated Parmesan cheese

2 garlic cloves, minced

¼ teaspoon salt

¼ teaspoon black pepper

Yields 1 cup

In a small bowl, use a hand mixer or whisk together all ingredients until smooth.

DIJON DILL DRESSING

½ cup Dijon mustard

½ cup red wine vinegar

1½ teaspoons dried tarragon

1½ teaspoons dill weed

2 cups olive oil

2 tablespoons freshly grated Parmesan cheese

2 tablespoons half and half

Yields 3½ cups

Blend all ingredients in a food processor until smooth.

FRENCH MUSTARD DRESSING

1½ cups olive oil

1 pint Dijon mustard

1 teaspoon garlic clove, minced

2 tablespoons onion, finely chopped

2 teaspoons fresh parsley, finely chopped

¾ teaspoon dried thyme

1 teaspoon dried tarragon

¼ teaspoon salt

½ teaspoon black pepper

Yields 1 quart

Beat oil into mustard slowly. Add remaining ingredients and refrigerate for 1 hour.

LEMON MUSTARD VINAIGRETTE

2 cups olive oil

2 tablespoons Dijon mustard

⅔ cup fresh lemon juice

3 garlic cloves, minced

1 tablespoon green onion, minced

¼ teaspoon salt

½ teaspoon white pepper

Yields 2 cups

Blend all ingredients in a food processor until smooth.

LEMON FRENCH DRESSING

1 cup olive oil
5 tablespoons fresh lemon juice
1 teaspoon lemon zest, finely grated
¼ teaspoon salt
¼ teaspoon black pepper

Yields 1 cup

In a bowl, use a hand mixer or a whisk to blend together all ingredients until smooth.

SPICY ORIENTAL DRESSING

1½ cups olive oil
3 tablespoons fresh lemon juice
4 tablespoons dry sherry
1 tablespoon Chinese mustard
2 tablespoons soy sauce
4 tablespoons sesame oil
¼ teaspoon cayenne pepper

Yields 2 cups

In a bowl, use a hand mixer or a whisk to blend together all ingredients until smooth.

ROQUEFORT DRESSING

¼ lb. Roquefort cheese, room temperature and crumbled

½ cup mayonnaise (see Index)

½ cup cream

½ cup sour cream

2 tablespoons fresh parsley, finely chopped

2 teaspoons Worcestershire sauce

2 tablespoons fresh lemon juice

2 teaspoons onion, finely chopped

½ teaspoon garlic powder

salt and pepper to taste

Yields 2 cups

In a food processor, combine all ingredients until well blended. Refrigerate for 1 hour. Serve immediately.

THOUSAND ISLAND DRESSING

2 cups mayonnaise (see Index)

½ cup catsup

1 tablespoon horseradish

1 tablespoon green pepper, finely chopped

2 tablespoons onion, finely chopped

1 hard-boiled egg, peeled and finely chopped

4 teaspoons fresh parsley, finely chopped

Yield 3 cups

In a bowl, use a hand mixer or a whisk to blend together all ingredients until smooth. Refrigerate for 2 hours before using.

TUNA CAPER DRESSING

6½ oz. canned white tuna, drained

1 cup mayonnaise (see Index)

2 teaspoons fresh lemon juice

1 tablespoon half and half

¼ teaspoon salt

¼ teaspoon black pepper

2 tablespoons capers, drained

Yield 1½ cups

Blend all ingredients in a food processor until smooth. Refrigerate for 2 hours before using.

BALSAMIC VINAIGRETTE

⅔ cup balsamic vinegar

1⅓ cups olive oil

2 tablespoons fresh lime juice

¼ teaspoon salt

¼ teaspoon white pepper

Yields 2 cups

In a bowl, use a hand mixer or a whisk to blend together all ingredients until smooth.

BASIL MINT VINAIGRETTE

½ cup fresh basil leaves

4 tablespoons fresh mint, finely chopped

4 garlic cloves, minced

1 cup olive oil

3 tablespoons freshly grated Parmesan cheese

2 tablespoons Dijon mustard

2 tablespoons anchovy paste

1 tablespoon fresh lime juice

¼ teaspoon salt

¼ teaspoon white pepper

3 dashes Tabasco®

Yields 1½ cups

In a food processor, combine all ingredients until smooth.

MUSTARD VINAIGRETTE DRESSING

2 tablespoons Dijon mustard

2 teaspoons fresh tarragon, finely chopped

2 tablespoons red wine vinegar

2 cups olive oil

½ teaspoon salt

½ teaspoon white pepper

Yields 2 cups

In a bowl, use a hand mixer or a whisk to blend together all ingredients until smooth.

GARLIC VINAIGRETTE

1⅓ cups olive oil

⅓ cup red wine vinegar

2 tablespoons garlic, minced

2 teaspoons salt

2 teaspoons black pepper

Yields 1½ cups

In a bowl, use a hand mixer or a whisk to blend together all ingredients until smooth.

CREAMY ITALIAN VINAIGRETTE

½ cup olive oil

½ cup red wine vinegar

2 tablespoons sour cream

1 tablespoon Dijon mustard

1 teaspoon fresh dill

2 green onions, minced

¼ teaspoon dried oregano

¼ teaspoon dried thyme

¼ teaspoon dried basil

3 tablespoons fresh lemon juice

1 teaspoon ground black pepper

Yields 1½ cups

In a food processor, combine all ingredients until smooth.

RED WINE VINAIGRETTE

½ cup red wine vinegar

2 cups olive oil

3 garlic cloves, minced

2 teaspoons Dijon mustard

¼ teaspoon salt

¼ teaspoon white pepper

Yields 2½ cups

In a food processor, combine all ingredients until smooth.

TARRAGON CAPER VINAIGRETTE

½ cup tarragon vinegar

⅓ cup capers, drained and minced

1¼ cups olive oil

¼ cup fresh lemon juice

¼ teaspoon salt

¼ teaspoon white pepper

Yields 2½ cups

In a food processor, combine all ingredients until smooth.

TARRAGON SHERRY VINAIGRETTE

2 teaspoons dried tarragon

2 tablespoons dill pickle relish

2 cups olive oil

¼ cup fresh lemon juice

⅓ cup sherry wine vinegar

2 tablespoons Dijon mustard

¼ teaspoon salt

¼ teaspoon black pepper

Yields 3 cups

In a food processor, combine all ingredients until smooth.

Mayonnaises

HOMEMADE MAYONNAISE

2 egg yolks

½ teaspoon salt

1 teaspoon lemon juice

½ teaspoon dry mustard

Pinch of cayenne

2 cups olive oil

2 tablespoons boiling water

Yields 2¼ cups

Combine the egg yolks, salt, lemon juice, dry mustard, and cayenne in a mixing bowl; beat with an electric mixer or whisk until slightly thickened, about 5 minutes. Add 1 cup of the oil a teaspoon at a time, beating constantly, until the mixture becomes a thick emulsion. Add the remaining 1 cup of oil, 1 to 2 tablespoons at a time. When all of the oil is incorporated, beat in 2 tablespoons boiling water. Cover and refrigerate until ready to use.

SPICY MAYONNAISE

2 egg yolks
½ teaspoon salt
1 teaspoon lemon juice
½ teaspoon dry mustard
⅛ teaspoon cayenne pepper
1 teaspoon Tabasco®
2 cups olive oil
2 tablespoons boiling water

Yields 2¼ cups

Combine the egg yolks, salt, lemon juice, dry mustard, cayenne, and Tabasco® in a mixing bowl; beat with an electric mixer or whisk until slightly thickened, about 5 minutes. Add 1 cup of the oil a teaspoon at a time, beating constantly, until the mixture becomes a thick emulsion. Add the remaining 1 cup of oil, 1to 2 tablespoons at a time. When all of the oil is incorporated, beat in 2 tablespoons of boiling water. Cover and refrigerate until ready to use.

ANCHOVY BASIL MAYONNAISE

1 cup mayonnaise (see Index)
6 garlic cloves, minced
1 teaspoon anchovy paste
4 tablespoons fresh parsley, finely chopped
1 tablespoon fresh basil, finely chopped
¼ teaspoon white pepper

Yields 1 cup

Blend all ingredients together in a food processor. Cover and refrigerate until ready to use.

DIJON MAYONNAISE

1 cup mayonnaise (see Index)

1 tablespoon Dijon mustard

3 dashes Tabasco®

¼ teaspoon salt

2 tablespoons capers, drained and minced

Yields 1 cup

Blend all ingredients together in a food processor. Cover and refrigerate until ready to use.

DILL MAYONNAISE

1 cup mayonnaise (see Index)

1 tablespoon fresh dill, finely chopped

2 garlic cloves, minced

1 green onion, finely chopped

¼ teaspoon white pepper

Yields 1¼ cups

Blend all ingredients together in a food processor. Cover and refrigerate until ready to use.

HERBED MAYONNAISE

2 cups mayonnaise (see Index)

4 tablespoons sour cream

1 teaspoon lemon juice

2 tablespoons fresh parsley, finely chopped

1 tablespoon fresh tarragon, finely chopped

3 teaspoons capers, finely chopped

¼ teaspoon salt

¼ teaspoon black pepper

Yields 2½ cups

Blend all ingredients together in a food processor. Cover and refrigerate until ready to use.

TARRAGON MAYONNAISE

1 cup mayonnaise (see Index)

2 tablespoons red wine vinegar

4 oz. cream cheese, room temperature

1 tablespoon fresh tarragon, finely chopped

Yields 1½ cups

Blend all ingredients together in a food processor. Cover and refrigerate until ready to use.

WATERCRESS MAYONNAISE

1 cup mayonnaise
3 tablespoons watercress leaves, finely chopped
1 green onion, finely chopped
1 tablespoon fresh lemon juice
¼ teaspoon salt
¼ teaspoon white pepper

Yields 1½ cups

Blend all ingredients together in a food processor. Cover and refrigerate until ready to use.

EASY ONE DISH MEALS

BAKED TROUT WITH VEGETABLES

4   8 oz. Trout fillets

½ cup (1 stick) butter or margarine, melted

½ teaspoon salt

½ teaspoon black pepper

2 teaspoons garlic, minced

1 cup onion, chopped

1 cup celery, chopped

2 cups fresh mushrooms, sliced

1 small zucchini, sliced and chopped

16 oz. tomato sauce

1 teaspoon lemon zest, finely grated

2 tablespoons Worcestershire sauce

⅛ teaspoon cayenne pepper

Preheat oven to 450° F.

Serves four

    In a greased baking pan, place the fish; brush with ¼ cup of the melted butter or margarine. Sprinkle the fish with ¼ teaspoon of the salt and ¼ teaspoon of the black pepper. Bake, uncovered about 12 to 14 minutes. In a saucepan, melt the remaining ¼ cup of melted butter or margarine; until tender, sauté the garlic, onion, celery, mushrooms, and zucchini. Then add the tomato sauce, the lemon zest, the remaining ¼ teaspoon salt, ¼ teaspoon of black pepper, the Worcestershire, and cayenne pepper. Bring to a boil; then reduce the heat, cover, and simmer for 6 to 10 minutes. Top the baked fish fillets with the vegetable mixture and serve.

REDFISH CHILI

1 large onion, sliced	
1 cup green pepper, finely chopped	
2 garlic cloves, minced	
3 tablespoons butter or margarine	
1½ teaspoons salt	
1½ teaspoons chili powder	
½ teaspoon oregano	
½ teaspoon black pepper	
16 oz. canned red kidney beans, undrained	
15 oz. canned whole tomatoes, undrained	
6 oz. tomato paste	
4 dashes Tabasco®	
4 8 oz. Redfish fillets, cut into pieces	

Serves four

In a Dutch oven, sauté the onion, green pepper, and garlic in butter or margarine until tender. Stir in the salt, chili powder, oregano, and black pepper. Add the kidney beans, tomatoes, tomato paste, and Tabasco.® Simmer over heat, stirring occasionally. Add the Redfish; cover, and reduce the heat. Gently simmer the fish for about 12 to 14 minutes and serve.

TAMPICO SHRIMP AND BLACK BEAN CHILI

3 tablespoons olive oil
1 green bell pepper, chopped
1 red bell pepper, chopped
1 large onion, chopped
2 tablespoons jalapeno peppers, finely chopped
1 teaspoon garlic, minced
1 tablespoon chili powder
1½ teaspoons dried cumin
16 oz. canned whole tomatoes, undrained and chopped
16 oz. canned black beans, rinsed and drained
¾ cup water
1½ lbs. raw shrimp, peeled and deveined

Serves four

In a large pot, heat the olive oil; sauté the green and red bell peppers, onion, jalapenos, and garlic until tender. Stir in the chili powder, cumin, tomatoes, black beans, water, and shrimp; bring to a boil. Reduce the heat and cook for about 10 to 12 minutes.

SHRIMP AEGEAN

3 tablespoons olive oil
1½ lbs. raw shrimp, peeled and deveined
1 cup onion, finely chopped
3 teaspoons garlic, minced
29 oz. canned tomatoes, drained and chopped
½ cup dry white wine
1 tablespoon fresh lemon juice
1 teaspoon salt
½ teaspoon ground black pepper
¼ teaspoon cayenne pepper
¾ lb. Feta cheese, crumbled
Preheat oven to 400° F.

Serves four

In a large oven-proof skillet, heat the oil, and sauté the shrimp until pink. Remove the shrimp and place on a platter. Add the onion and garlic to the skillet; cook until tender. Add the tomatoes, white wine, lemon juice, salt, black pepper, and cayenne pepper; stir and bring to a boil. Cook for about 8 minutes; then place the shrimp on top of the tomato sauce. Sprinkle on the Feta cheese and bake for about 15 minutes.

SHRIMP SALAD LETTUCE WRAPS

1 lb. cooked shrimp, deveined and chopped
6 tablespoons mayonnaise (see Index)
4 hard-boiled eggs, peeled and chopped
1 cup celery, chopped
2 tablespoons fresh parsley, chopped
1 cup green onion, finely chopped
1 tablespoon lemon juice
½ teaspoon dry mustard
½ teaspoon Tabasco®
½ teaspoon garlic powder
½ teaspoon salt
½ teaspoon black pepper
⅛ teaspoon cayenne pepper
6 large iceberg lettuce leaves

Serves six

Mix all the ingredients together well, except for the lettuce leaves. On a plate, place the 6 lettuce leaves. Into each of the leaves, drop ⅙ of the shrimp mixture. Roll up like a taco and serve.

BLACKENED REDFISH SALAD

1 tablespoon cayenne pepper
1 tablespoon black pepper
1 tablespoon plus ½ teaspoon white pepper
1½ teaspoons salt
6 Redfish fillets, 6 to 8 oz. each (Drum or Trout can be substituted.)
1 cup Worcestershire sauce
1¼ cups peanut oil
1¼ cups red wine vinegar
1½ cups chopped pecans
1 tablespoon vegetable oil
3 heads romaine lettuce, chopped into bite-size pieces
1½ cups green onion, chopped
3 heads Belgian endive, sliced diagonally
Preheat oven to 350° F.

Serves six

In a small bowl, combine the cayenne, black pepper, 1 tablespoon of the white pepper, and ½ teaspoon of the salt (or less according to taste). Set the seasoning mixture aside.

Place the Redfish in a shallow dish and pour the Worcestershire sauce over the fillets. Marinate the fish for 30 minutes in the refrigerator, turning the fish several times.

In a medium bowl or cruet, combine the peanut oil and vinegar with the remaining ½ teaspoon of white pepper and 1 teaspoon salt. Whisk until well blended, then set the dressing aside.

Spread the pecans in a single layer on a rimmed baking sheet and roast in the hot oven about 8 minutes. Let cool.

Sprinkle the marinated fillets on both sides with the seasoning mixture. Coat a large cast iron skillet with the oil and heat until almost smoking. Place the Redfish in the hot skillet and sear about 2 minutes per side, until the seasoning mixture has melted into the fish. Remove from the skillet and break or cut into bite-size pieces.

In a large bowl, combine the romaine, green onion, endive, and blackened Redfish. Add dressing as desired and toss until the ingredients are well coated.

Mound blackened Redfish salad on six chilled plates and garnish with roasted pecans.

GRILLED CHICKEN CAESAR SALAD

3 heads romaine lettuce

6 whole boneless, skinless chicken breasts (see note below)

3 cups Quick Caesar dressing (see Index)

1 cup freshly grated Romano cheese

Salt and black pepper

Heat a grill or broiler.

Serves six

Wash the romaine lettuce and chop the leaves into bite-size pieces. Place the chopped lettuce in a large bowl.

Season the chicken breasts on both sides with salt and pepper, then grill or broil the chicken until completely cooked, about 5 to 7 minutes per side. Cut the breasts into bite-size pieces and add the pieces to the bowl with the Romaine lettuce; then toss the salad.

Pour the Caesar dressing over the salad and toss until the ingredients are well coated. Mound the salad onto six chilled plates and sprinkle with Romano cheese. If desired, garnish with cherry tomatoes, wedges of boiled egg, radishes, or assorted pickled vegetables.

Note: 6 salmon fillets, about 6 to 8 oz. each, can be substituted
  for the chicken.

CUCUMBER CHICKEN LETTUCE WRAPS

½ cup plain yogurt

¼ cup cucumber, peeled and finely chopped

¼ teaspoon dried dill

¼ teaspoon dried mint

4 large iceberg lettuce leaves

4 skinless, boneless chicken breasts, cooked and sliced

1 tomato, thinly sliced

⅓ cup Feta cheese, crumbled

Serves four

In a small bowl, stir together the yogurt, cucumber, dill, and mint; set aside. On a plate, place the 4 lettuce leaves. Inside each leaf, drop ¼ of the mixture, then the chicken, next the tomato, and on top the Feta cheese. Roll up like a taco and serve.

PARMESAN DIJON CHICKEN

¾ cup bread crumbs (see Index)

¼ cup freshly grated Parmesan cheese

⅔ cup butter or margarine, melted

3 tablespoons Dijon mustard

⅛ teaspoon salt

½ teaspoon black pepper

3 tablespoons olive oil

6 skinned, boneless chicken breasts

20 oz. frozen chopped spinach, cooked

Preheat oven to 375° F.

Serves six

In a bowl, mix the bread crumbs and cheese. In another bowl, combine the butter or margarine, mustard, salt, and pepper. Dip the chicken in the butter or margarine mixture and coat well with the bread crumb and cheese mixture. Pour the olive oil in a baking dish. Cover the bottom of the dish with the cooked spinach and top with the chicken. Bake uncovered, for about 40 minutes.

LEMON AND FRESH DILL CHICKEN

⅓ cup butter or margarine
6 skinned, boneless chicken breasts
¾ cup chicken broth or stock (see Index)
1½ tablespoons fresh dill, chopped
1½ tablespoons fresh lemon juice
1½ teaspoons salt
3 tablespoons green onion, chopped

Serves six

In a skillet, melt the butter or margarine; cook the chicken about 8 minutes, turning once. In a bowl, mix the chicken broth or stock, fresh dill, lemon juice, and salt. Heat to a boil and reduce the heat to low. Cover and simmer for 25 to 30 minutes. Place the chicken on a serving platter and keep warm. Meanwhile, bring the broth or stock mixture to a boil and cook for about 4 to 5 minutes. Pour over the chicken; sprinkle the chicken with the green onion and serve over cooked brown rice.

SAFFRON CHICKEN AND BROWN RICE

1 4lbs. chicken, cut into pieces
1 tablespoon salt
½ teaspoon ground black pepper
4 tablespoons olive oil
1 cup onion, chopped
1 cup green bell pepper, chopped
1 cup red bell pepper, chopped
2 teaspoons garlic, minced
¼ lb. ham, chopped
1½ cups uncooked brown rice
4 cups chicken broth or stock (see Index)
1 teaspoon paprika
½ teaspoon saffron
1 bay leaf
1 cup peas
Preheat oven to 375° F.

Serves four

Season the chicken with the salt and pepper. In a large oven-proof skillet, heat the olive oil on medium-high heat and brown the chicken. Remove the chicken from the skillet and place on the side. Reduce the heat to medium; add the onions, red and green bell peppers, garlic, ham and sauté until tender. Add the brown rice and stir to combine all the ingredients. Pour in the broth or stock and bring to a boil. Reduce the heat to medium-low; stir in the paprika, saffron, and bay leaf. Return the chicken to the skillet; cover and bake for 40 minutes. Add the peas; cover and bake for an 10 additional minutes.

WHITE BEAN AND CHICKEN CHILI

3 tablespoons butter or margarine

1½ cups onion, chopped

3 garlic cloves, minced

4 cups cooked chicken breast, chopped

¾ teaspoon ground cumin

20 oz. medium salsa

16 oz. canned great northern beans, rinsed and drained

4 tablespoons sour cream

Serves four

In a Dutch oven, over medium-high heat, cook the onion and garlic in the butter or margarine until tender. Stir in the remaining ingredients, except the sour cream. Heat to a boil; reduce the heat to low. Simmer, uncovered, for 4 to 5 minutes, stirring occasionally until well heated. Top each serving with a dollop of sour cream.

CHICKEN AND FRESH MUSHROOMS

2 tablespoons olive oil

1 tablespoon butter or margarine

4 skinned, boneless chicken breasts

1 teaspoon salt

½ teaspoon ground black pepper

2 cups green onion, chopped

4 cups fresh mushrooms, sliced

1 cup celery, chopped

2 teaspoons garlic, minced

1 teaspoon dried thyme

¾ cup dry white wine

Serves four

In a large skillet, over medium-high heat, add the olive oil and butter or margarine. Add the chicken with the salt and pepper and brown for about 5 minutes. Remove the chicken and place on the side. Sauté the green onion, mushrooms, celery, and garlic until tender. Add the thyme and white wine, stirring constantly. Bring to a boil; reduce the heat, cover, and simmer for 15 minutes. Add the chicken; cover, and cook for 25 to 30 minutes. Can be served over cooked brown rice.

CHICKEN AND BARLEY STEW

3 tablespoons olive oil

1½ cups onion, chopped

1½ cups celery, chopped

1 cup fresh mushrooms, sliced

3 teaspoons garlic, minced

6 cups chicken broth or stock (see Index)

1 cup canned tomatoes, drained and chopped

1 cup pearl barley

1 lb. skinned, boneless chicken breast, cut into pieces

1 teaspoon salt

1 teaspoon ground black pepper

Serves four

In a large pot, over medium-high heat, add the oil and sauté the onions, celery, mushrooms, and garlic until tender. Stir in the broth or stock with the tomatoes and bring to a boil. Add the barley and continue stirring. Reduce the heat and simmer for 30 minutes. Place the pieces of chicken into the pot and cook for an additional 30 to 35 minutes. Sprinkle with the salt and pepper, then serve.

SWEET POTATO AND CHICKEN HASH

4 skinned, boneless chicken breasts, cooked and chopped
1½ lbs. sweet potatoes, cooked and chopped
3 tablespoons butter or margarine
1 large onion, finely chopped
1 small red bell pepper, finely chopped
4 garlic cloves, minced
1 teaspoon paprika
½ teaspoon ground black pepper
½ teaspoon dried thyme
½ teaspoon salt
½ cup green onion, chopped
¼ cup fresh parsley, chopped
1 cup half and half

Serves four

In a heavy skillet, warm the butter or margarine; sauté the onion, red bell pepper, and garlic until tender. Add the spices and salt; cook for about 1 additional minute. Stir in the chicken, sweet potatoes, green onion, parsley, and half and half; cook, stirring until the half and half reduces slightly and hash thickens.

TURKEY AND BROWN RICE

| 3 tablespoons olive oil |
| 1 lb. ground turkey |
| 1 cup onion, chopped |
| 1 cup green onion, chopped |
| ¾ cup uncooked brown rice |
| 2 teaspoons chili powder |
| 1½ cups chicken broth or stock (see Index) |
| 1 teaspoon salt |
| ½ teaspoon ground cumin |
| 1 teaspoon ground black pepper |
| 8 oz. tomato sauce |
| 15 oz. canned whole tomatoes, drained and chopped |

Serves four

In a large skillet, heat the olive oil over medium-high heat. Add the turkey, onion, and green pepper. Cook until the turkey is browned and drain. Stir in the remaining ingredients; reduce the heat, cover, and simmer for 25 to 30 minutes.

CREAMED TURKEY AND BROCCOLI

12 oz. turkey breast, cooked and chopped

6 cups broccoli, cooked

1 lb. whole grain spaghetti, cooked and chopped

12 oz. cream cheese, room temperature

1 tablespoon garlic, minced

1 cup milk

1 teaspoon ground black pepper

Serves four

In a Dutch oven, combine the cream cheese, garlic, milk, and pepper. Cook and stir over low heat until the cream cheese is melted. Add the pasta, broccoli, and turkey. Toss the ingredients until coated with the cheese mixture, then serve.

BEEF BURRITO LETTUCE WRAPS

2 tablespoons olive oil

1 cup onion, finely chopped

2 teaspoons garlic, mined

1¼ lbs. ground beef

1 tablespoon chili powder

1 teaspoon ground cumin

1 teaspoon salt

1¼ cups chunky medium salsa

¼ lb. sharp Cheddar cheese, finely grated

4 large iceberg lettuce leaves

Serves four

In a large skillet, over medium-high heat, add the olive oil; sauté the onions and garlic until tender. Add the beef, chili powder, cumin, and salt. Cook until all the beef is browned; then drain. Add the salsa, and cook about 5 minutes. Remove from the heat and stir in the cheese. Spoon ¼ of the beef mixture into the center of each lettuce leaf. Fold like a taco and serve.

BEEF AND BLACK BEANS

1½ lbs. lean beef, cut into 1 inch cubes
2 tablespoons olive oil
1 tablespoon fresh parsley, chopped
1 cup green pepper, chopped
½ cup onion, chopped
½ cup green onion, finely chopped
1 cup tomato sauce
1 tablespoon white wine vinegar
2 tablespoons Worcestershire sauce
½ teaspoon salt
¼ teaspoon black pepper
¼ teaspoon Tabasco®
30 oz. canned black beans, rinsed and drained

Serves four

In a skillet, over medium heat, add the oil; add the beef and cook until desired doneness. Stir in the parsley, green pepper, and onions; sauté until tender. Add the remaining ingredients, stirring frequently until hot. Can be served over cooked brown rice.

BLACK BEAN AND BROWN RICE BURGERS

30 oz. canned black beans, rinsed and drained
2 cups cooked brown rice
½ cup onion, finely chopped
1½ teaspoons garlic powder
½ teaspoon salt
½ teaspoon black pepper
6 tablespoons medium salsa
3 tablespoons olive oil

Serves four

In a bowl, mash the beans and mix with the brown rice, onion, garlic powder, salt, pepper, and salsa. In a skillet, heat the oil; form the bean mixture into ½ inch thick patties (about ½ cup per patty). Place the patties in the skillet and cook 5 minutes on each side; remove and serve.

BLACK-EYED PEAS

2 lbs. dried Black-Eyed Peas
5 quarts water
⅓ cup olive oil
6 stalks celery, finely chopped
2 large onions, finely chopped
2 medium green peppers, finely chopped
2 tablespoons garlic, minced
4 tablespoons margarine or butter
1 tablespoon salt
2 tablespoons garlic powder
black or crushed red pepper to taste
1½ lbs. sausage or ham, cut into 1 inch pieces

Serves eight to ten

Rinse peas in a colander 3 or 4 times. Sauté chopped seasoning in olive oil until soft. Add rinsed peas to water. Bring to a boil and cook for 15 to 20 minutes. Reduce to low-medium heat and cook until peas are soft. Add the margarine or butter and cook until the peas reach a creamy consistency, about 30 to 45 minutes. Brown ham or sausage, in a skillet and add to peas; pepper to taste. Serve immediately over cooked brown rice.

ITALIAN MELT

3 tablespoons olive oil

3 garlic cloves, minced

15 oz. canned tomatoes, finely chopped

¼ teaspoon dried oregano

½ teaspoon dried basil

¼ teaspoon salt

¼ teaspoon black pepper

4 4 oz. slices Provolone cheese

Serves four

In a large skillet, heat the olive oil and sauté the garlic until tender. Add the tomatoes, oregano, basil, salt, and pepper. Reduce the heat and simmer for about 15 to 20 minutes, stirring occasionally. Arrange the cheese slices over the tomato mixture; cover and cook over low heat, about 4 minutes until cheese begins to melt.

BASIC OMELETTE

4 large eggs

⅛ teaspoon salt

⅛ teaspoon black pepper

3 tablespoons butter or margarine

Serves two

In a small bowl, beat the eggs, salt, and pepper with a fork until blended. Melt the butter or margarine in an 8-inch skillet or omelette pan. Pour in the egg mixture and stir briskly. Cook the eggs over low heat; lift the edges of the omelette and shake the pan several times during cooking to keep the eggs from sticking. When the eggs are firm and the bottom is light brown, fold the omelette over and transfer it to a heated plate.

CHEESE OMELETTE

4 eggs

⅛ teaspoon salt

⅛ teaspoon black pepper

3 tablespoons butter or margarine

¾ cup Cheddar cheese, grated

Serves two

In a small bowl, beat the eggs, salt, and pepper with a fork until blended. Melt the butter or margarine in an 8-inch skillet or omelette pan, then add the egg mixture, stirring briskly. Cook the eggs over low heat; lift the edges of the omelette and shake the pan several times during cooking to keep the eggs from sticking. When the eggs are almost set, fold in the cheese. Cook until the bottom forms a golden crust, then fold the omelette over and transfer it to a heated plate.

SWISS AND CRABMEAT OMELETTE

4 eggs

⅛ teaspoon salt

⅛ teaspoon black pepper

3 tablespoons butter or margarine

¾ cup lump crabmeat, picked over to remove any shell or cartilage

¾ cup Swiss cheese, grated

Serves two

In a small bowl, beat the eggs, salt, and pepper with a fork until blended. Melt the butter or margarine in an 8-inch skillet or omelette pan, then add the egg mixture and crabmeat, stirring briskly. Cook the eggs over low heat; lift the edges of the omelette and shake the pan several times during cooking to keep the eggs from sticking. When the eggs are almost set, fold in the cheese. Cook until the bottom forms a golden crust, then fold the omelette over and transfer it to a heated plate.

OMELETTE WITH FINE HERBS

4 large eggs

⅛ teaspoon salt

⅛ teaspoon black pepper

3 tablespoons butter or margarine

2 tablespoons green onion, finely chopped

1 tablespoon fresh oregano, finely chopped

1 tablespoon fresh parsley, finely chopped

Serves two

In a small bowl, beat the eggs, salt, and pepper with a fork until blended. Melt the butter or margarine in an 8-inch skillet or omelette pan, then add the egg mixture and fresh herbs, stirring briskly. Cook the eggs over low heat; lift the edges of the omelette and shake the pan several times during cooking to keep the eggs from sticking. Cook until the bottom forms a golden crust, then fold the omelette over and transfer it to a heated plate.

Note: Marjoram, thyme, basil, or any combination of fresh herbs can flavor the omelette.

FRESH MUSHROOM OMELETTE

4 large eggs

⅛ teaspoon salt

⅛ teaspoon black pepper

3 tablespoons butter or margarine

¾ cup sliced fresh mushrooms

Serves two

In a small bowl, beat the eggs, salt, and pepper with a fork until blended. Melt the butter or margarine in an 8-inch skillet or omelette pan, then add the egg mixture and mushrooms, stirring briskly. Cook the eggs over low heat; lift the edges of the omelette and shake the pan several times during cooking to keep the eggs from sticking. Cook until the bottom forms a golden crust, then fold the omelette over and transfer it to a heated plate to serve.

SHRIMP OMELETTE

¾ cup boiled shrimp, peeled, deveined, and chopped

4 large eggs

⅛ teaspoon salt

⅛ teaspoon black pepper

3 tablespoons butter or margarine

Serves two

In a small bowl, beat the eggs, salt, and pepper with a fork until blended. Melt the butter or margarine in an 8-inch skillet or omelette pan, then add the egg mixture and shrimp, stirring briskly. Cook the eggs over low heat; lift the edges of the omelette and shake the pan several times during cooking to keep the eggs from sticking. Cook until the bottom forms a golden crust, then fold the omelette over and transfer it to a heated plate to serve.

CRUSTLESS QUICHE CHICKEN FLORENTINE

2 cups chicken breast, cooked and chopped

8 oz. Mozzarella cheese, shredded

½ cup heavy cream

⅓ cup pesto sauce

10 oz. frozen spinach, thawed and drained

6 eggs

2 cups pasta sauce

Preheat oven to 375° F.

Serves six

Grease a 9 inch glass dish. Mix 1½ cups of the cheese, the heavy cream, pesto, spinach, and eggs until well blended. Pour into the glass dish. Bake for about 30 minutes; sprinkle with the remaining cheese and bake until the cheese is melted. Meanwhile, in a small saucepan, heat the pasta sauce, and add the chicken until well heated. To serve, cut the quiche into portions and top with the pasta sauce mixture.

QUICHE PIE CRUST

2 cups stone ground whole wheat pastry flour

½ teaspoon salt

Dash of Ki-Sweet or granulated Sweet 'N Low®

½ cup (1 stick) cold butter or margarine

2 - 3 tablespoons shortening

5 tablespoons cold water

Preheat oven to 400° F.

Yields one pie shell

Place all ingredients, except water, in a mixing bowl. Combine mixture with your hands, until mixture has formed into a smooth ball. Place ball into bowl and put into refrigerator for several hours or into the freezer for 45 minutes. Place on a wooden counter or cutting board, and using a rolling pin, flatten the dough, to about ⅛ inch thick. Place the flattened dough into a 10 inch baking dish and cover with wax paper. Use dried beans to hold the paper down. Bake pie crust for 8 to 10 minutes.

CRABMEAT AND CHEDDAR CHEESE QUICHE

4 tablespoons butter or margarine
3 large onions, finely chopped
3 cloves garlic, minced
6 eggs, beaten
2 egg yolks, beaten
1¼ cup half and half
1 cup whipping cream
12 oz. lump crabmeat
¾ lb. Cheddar cheese, grated
2 - 3 tablespoons fresh parsley, finely chopped
½ teaspoon nutmeg
1½ teaspoons salt
1¼ teaspoons black pepper
Quiche Pie Crust (see Index)
Preheat oven to 350° F.

Serves six to eight

Melt butter or margarine in a pan and sauté garlic and onion, until a golden brown; let cool. In a mixing bowl, beat the eggs, egg yolks, half and half and whipping cream. Fold the crabmeat and cheese into the batter with the onion and garlic mixture. Add parsley, nutmeg, pepper, and salt to batter. Pour batter into the partially cooked pie shell and bake for 30 minutes or until a toothpick comes out clean.

SMOKED SALMON AND GOAT CHEESE QUICHE

4 tablespoons butter or margarine
3 large onions, finely chopped
3 cloves garlic, minced
6 eggs, beaten
2 egg yolks, beaten
1¼ cup half and half
1 cup whipping cream
12 oz. smoked salmon, chopped
¾ lb. goat cheese, grated
2 - 3 tablespoons fresh parsley, finely chopped
½ teaspoon nutmeg
1½ teaspoons salt
1¼ teaspoons black pepper
Quiche Pie Crust (see Index)
Preheat oven to 350° F.

Serves six to eight

Melt butter or margarine in a pan and sauté garlic and onion, until a golden brown; let cool. In a mixing bowl, beat the eggs, egg yolks, half and half, and whipping cream. Fold the salmon and goat cheese into the batter with the onion and garlic mixture. Add parsley, nutmeg, pepper, and salt to batter. Pour batter into the partially cooked pie shell and bake for 30 minutes or until a toothpick comes out clean.

CORNED BEEF AND SWISS CHEESE QUICHE

1 lb. corned beef, cooked and chopped

4 tablespoons butter or margarine

3 large onions, finely chopped

3 cloves garlic, minced

6 eggs, beaten

2 egg yolks, beaten

1¼ cup half and half

1 cup whipping cream

¾ lb. Swiss cheese, grated

2 - 3 tablespoons fresh parsley, finely chopped

½ teaspoon nutmeg

1½ teaspoons salt

1¼ teaspoons black pepper

Quiche Pie Crust (see Index)

Preheat oven to 350° F.

Serves six to eight

Melt butter or margarine in a pan and sauté garlic and onion, until a golden brown; let cool. In a mixing bowl, beat the eggs, egg yolks, half and half, and whipping cream. Fold the corned beef and cheese into the batter with the onion and garlic mixture. Add parsley, nutmeg, pepper, and salt to batter. Pour batter into the partially cooked pie shell and bake for 30 minutes or until a toothpick comes out clean.

ITALIAN QUICHE

4 tablespoons butter or margarine

3 large onions, finely chopped

3 cloves garlic, minced

6 eggs, beaten

2 egg yolks, beaten

1¼ cups half and half

1 cup whipping cream

1 cup tomato, chopped

¾ lb. Mozzarella cheese, grated

½ cup pesto

2 - 3 tablespoons fresh parsley, finely chopped

½ teaspoon nutmeg

1½ teaspoons salt

1¼ teaspoons black pepper

Quiche Pie Crust (see Index)

Preheat oven to 350° F.

Serves six to eight

Melt butter or margarine in a pan and sauté garlic and onion, until a golden brown; let cool. In a mixing bowl, beat the eggs, egg yolks, half and half, and whipping cream. Fold the tomato and cheese into the batter with the onion and garlic mixture. Add pesto, parsley, nutmeg, pepper, and salt to batter. Pour batter into the partially cooked pie shell and bake for 30 minutes or until a toothpick comes out clean.

SWEET POTATO PANCAKES

1 large egg

1½ cups milk

⅓ cup cooking oil

2 tablespoons sweet potato, cooked and mashed

2 cups stone ground whole wheat flour

1 teaspoon salt

4 teaspoons baking soda

Serves four

Beat egg well. Add milk, oil and sweet potato; blend well. Mix flour, salt, and baking soda. Add to egg and beat mixture vigorously. Heat a skillet, coat with cooking oil of your choice. Drop the mixture by tablespoons into the hot oil. Brown pancakes on both sides, then drain on paper towels. Serve with butter or margarine and sugar-free syrup.

ALMOND OATMEAL WAFFLE

4 tablespoons oatmeal
2 tablespoons stone ground whole wheat flour
¼ teaspoon Ki-Sweet or ½ teaspoon granulated Sweet 'N Low®
1 teaspoon baking soda
2 dashes salt
2 large eggs, separated
½ cup milk
¼ teaspoon almond extract
½ oz. almonds, finely chopped

Serves two

In a small bowl combine oatmeal, flour, sugar substitute, baking soda, and salt. In another small bowl whisk together egg yolk, milk, almond extract, and almonds. Stir into oatmeal mixture until just combined. Set aside. In a separate small bowl, with electric mixer on high speed, beat egg whites until stiff; fold into oatmeal mixture. Pour batter into preheated waffle iron. Close and bake on high, about 4 minutes, until golden brown. Serve immediately.

ENTRÉES

RED SNAPPER PARMESAN

1 cup sour cream
⅓ cup freshly grated Parmesan cheese
1 tablespoon fresh lemon juice
1 hard-boiled egg, peeled and finely chopped
½ teaspoon salt
1½ cups sour cream
4 dashes Tabasco®
1 small tomato, finely chopped
1 small onion, finely chopped
2 lbs. Red Snapper fillets
Preheat oven to 350° F.

Serves four

In a large bowl, mix all ingredients, except the Red Snapper, into a smooth creamy mixture. Place the Red Snapper in a single layer onto a greased baking dish. Spoon the mixture over the fish and bake for 20 to 30 minutes.

FLOUNDER WITH LEMON BUTTER SAUCE

½ cup (1 stick) butter or margarine
1 teaspoon dried dill
1 teaspoon dried thyme
2 green onions, thinly sliced
2 tablespoons fresh lemon juice
2 lbs. Flounder fillets

Serves four

In a large skillet, melt the butter or margarine and sauté the dill, thyme, green onions, and lemon juice. Add the Flounder fillets and cook over medium heat for 4 to 6 minutes on each side or until each side is brown. Place the Flounder on a serving platter; pour the lemon butter sauce over the fillets, and serve.

SPICY CATFISH WITH PECANS

½ cup stone ground whole wheat flour

4 tablespoons bread crumbs (see Index)

2 teaspoons chili powder

1 teaspoon garlic salt

2 lbs. Catfish fillets, ½ to 1 inch thick

6 tablespoons butter or margarine

½ cup pecans, chopped

2 tablespoons fresh lemon juice

¼ teaspoon cayenne pepper

Serves four

In a shallow dish, stir together flour, bread crumbs, chili powder, and garlic salt. Dip Catfish into the mixture. In a large skillet, cook the Catfish in 4 tablespoons of the butter or margarine over medium heat for 4 to 6 minutes on each side. Remove the Catfish from the skillet and keep warm. Melt the remaining 2 tablespoons butter or margarine in the skillet. Add the pecans and cook over medium heat for 3 to 5 minutes, while constantly stirring. Stir in lemon juice and cayenne pepper. Drizzle pecan mixture over Catfish fillets and serve.

DOVER SOLE AMANDINE

1 cup stone ground whole wheat flour

½ teaspoon black pepper

1 cup milk

4 Dover Sole fillets, about 8 oz. each

¾ cup (1½ sticks) butter or margarine

1 cup almonds, sliced and blanched

1 tablespoon fresh lemon juice

1 tablespoon fresh parsley, finely chopped

Serves four

In a shallow dish, combine the flour and pepper. Pour the milk into a separate dish. Dip the fillets in the milk, then into the flour mixture. In a large skillet, heat ¼ cup of the butter or margarine over medium-low heat; add half of the fillets and sauté, turning after 3 to 4 minutes or until the fillets are browned on both sides. Remove the fish and place on a serving platter. Repeat with the remaining fillets. Add the remaining butter or margarine, then add the almonds and brown. Stir in the lemon juice and parsley; then pour over the fish and serve.

BAKED TROUT WITH FRESH MUSHROOMS

4 Trout fillets, 8 oz. each

1 teaspoon salt

2 cups fresh mushrooms, sliced

1 large tomato, chopped

¾ teaspoon black pepper

1 cup Mozzarella cheese, shredded

3 tablespoons freshly grated Parmesan cheese

Preheat oven to 325° F.

Serves four

In a lightly greased baking dish, place the Trout and cover with the mushrooms, tomato, salt, and pepper. Cover and bake for about 25 minutes. Uncover and sprinkle with the cheeses; then cover and let stand until the cheeses are melted.

TROUT WITH MACADAMIA NUTS

2 eggs

2 tablespoons water

¼ teaspoon salt

¼ teaspoon white pepper

4 Trout fillets, 8 oz. each

8 oz. Macadamia nuts, finely chopped

3 tablespoons olive oil

4 tablespoons butter or margarine

2 tablespoons fresh lemon juice

2 tablespoons fresh parsley, finely chopped

Serves four

In a shallow dish, whip the eggs with the water, salt, and pepper. Coat the Trout with the egg mixture. Dredge the fillets in the nuts, coating both sides of the fish. In a skillet, sauté the fillets in olive oil on medium-high heat for 2 to 3 minutes on each side or until golden brown. Remove the fillets and place on a warm serving platter. In the same skillet, melt the butter or margarine until it begins to brown. Add lemon juice and chopped parsley; pour over fillets and serve.

SALMON WITH DILL SAUCE

4 tablespoons butter or margarine

1 cup half and half

¾ cup dry white wine

2 tablespoons fresh lemon juice

2 tablespoons fresh dill, chopped

4 Salmon fillets, 8 oz. each

Serves four

In a large skillet, melt the butter or margarine over high heat. Add all the ingredients except for the Salmon; stir well. Add the Salmon and reduce the heat to medium-low. Simmer for about 15 minutes, turning halfway through the cooking. Place the fillets on a platter, top with the sauce, then serve.

BAKED SALMON WITH FRESH BASIL

1 3 lbs. whole Salmon, cleaned with head and tail attached

4 cups fresh basil leaves, chopped

3 tablespoons olive oil

¾ cup onion, finely chopped

¼ teaspoon salt

¼ teaspoon black pepper

Preheat oven to 425° F.

Serves four

Stuff the Salmon with the fresh basil. Cover with the olive oil and sprinkle the onion, salt, and pepper over the Salmon. In aluminum foil, wrap the Salmon and refrigerate for about 2 hours. Bake the fish for about 40 minutes and serve.

SALMON WITH TARRAGON BUTTER

3 tablespoons butter or margarine, melted

2 teaspoons lime zest, finely grated

2 teaspoons fresh lime juice

2 teaspoons fresh tarragon, finely chopped

4 Salmon fillets, 8 oz. each

2 teaspoons butter or margarine, melted

Heat the broiler

Serves four

In a small bowl, stir together the 3 tablespoons butter or margarine, lime zest, lime juice, and tarragon; set aside. Place the Salmon on a lightly greased broiler pan. Baste with the 2 teaspoons melted butter or margarine. Broil for 8 to 12 minutes, turning once after half of the broiling time. Top each fillet with ¼ of the tarragon butter, then serve.

SALMON DIJON

4 Salmon fillets, 8 oz. each
4 tablespoons mayonnaise (see Index)
2 tablespoons Dijon mustard
2 teaspoons lemon pepper seasoning
Heat the broiler
Serves four

Place the Salmon on a lightly greased broiler pan. Broil for 8 to
12 minutes, turning once after half of the broiling time. In a small bowl, stir
together mayonnaise, mustard, and lemon pepper seasoning. Spread the
mixture over the fish. Broil for an additional 2 minutes until mustard
mixture is lightly brown and serve.

SEARED PEPPER TUNA

4 tablespoons ground black pepper
4 Tuna steaks, 8 oz. each, cut 1 inch thick
3 tablespoons olive oil
Serves four

Pepper the Tuna steaks on both sides. In a nonstick skillet, heat the olive
oil over medium-high heat. Add the Tuna and sear the first side for about
5 minutes. Turn the Tuna over and sear the other side for 3 minutes,
then serve.

STEAMED MUSSELS

16 oz. chicken broth or stock (see Index)

¾ cup dry white wine

2 tablespoons garlic, minced

1½ teaspoons salt

2 teaspoons black pepper

2 lbs. fresh mussels, cleaned

Serves four

In a large soup pot, combine the chicken broth or stock, white wine, garlic, salt, pepper, and bring to a boil. Add the mussels to the pot, cover, and cook for about 4 minutes until the mussels open. Do not overcook the mussels. Remove any mussels that do not open.

ITALIAN MUSSELS

2 tablespoons olive oil

2 tablespoons butter or margarine

4 garlic cloves, minced

1 medium onion, finely chopped

2 tablespoons fresh parsley, finely chopped

4 basil leaves, finely chopped

½ teaspoon dried oregano

2 teaspoons black pepper

36 fresh mussels, cleaned

1 cup dry white wine

Serves four

In a large soup pot, combine the olive oil, butter, garlic, onion, parsley, basil, oregano, and pepper. Stir and heat gently for 10 minutes. Add the mussels and wine. Cover, bring to a boil and allow to simmer for 8 minutes or until the shells open. Remove any mussels that do not open.

SPICY ITALIAN SHRIMP

29 oz. canned tomatoes, mashed

3 tablespoons red wine vinegar

1 teaspoon Italian seasoning

1 large green pepper, chopped

1 cup onion, chopped

2 lbs. raw shrimp, peeled and deveined

½ teaspoon cayenne pepper

Serves four

In a medium-sized saucepan, combine the tomatoes, vinegar, Italian seasoning, green pepper, and onion. Bring to a boil, then simmer over medium-low heat for 10 minutes. Reduce the heat to low. Add the shrimp and the cayenne pepper. Allow to simmer for an additional 10 minutes, until the shrimp are pink and completely cooked. Serve over cooked brown rice.

SPANISH SHRIMP

⅔ cup olive oil

8 garlic cloves, minced

2 bay leaves

1½ teaspoons Tabasco®

¼ teaspoon salt

2 lbs. raw shrimp, peeled and deveined

Serves four

In a large skillet, heat the oil over medium heat; stir in the garlic, bay leaf, Tabasco,® and salt. When the garlic softens, add the shrimp and cook for about 3 minutes until the shrimp are pink and completely cooked. Serve over cooked brown rice.

GARLIC SHRIMP

2 lbs. raw shrimp, peeled and deveined

3 tablespoons fresh parsley, chopped

5 teaspoons garlic, minced

¾ cup olive oil

¼ teaspoon salt

¼ teaspoon black pepper

Serves four

   In a medium-size bowl, toss the shrimp with the parsley and 4 of the teaspoons of garlic. Cover and refrigerate for 4 hours. In a large skillet, heat the olive oil over medium-high heat. Add the shrimp, remaining 1 teaspoon garlic, salt, and pepper. Cook for 4 to 5 minutes until shrimp are pink and completely cooked. Serve over cooked whole grain pasta.

SHRIMP PARMESAN

2 lbs. boiled shrimp, peeled and deveined

¼ teaspoon salt

¼ teaspoon black pepper

¾ lb. fresh mushrooms, sliced

10 tablespoons butter or margarine, room temperature

1 tablespoon stone ground whole wheat flour

2 cups sour cream

2 teaspoons soy sauce

½ cup freshly grated Parmesan cheese

2 teaspoons paprika

Preheat oven to 400° F.

Serves four

   In a greased shallow baking dish, place the shrimp in a single layer and sprinkle with the salt and pepper. In a medium-size skillet, sauté the mushrooms in 5 tablespoons of the butter or margarine. Transfer the mushrooms to a medium-size bowl and toss with the flour. Stir in the sour cream, the remaining 5 tablespoons butter or margarine, and soy sauce. Pour the mushroom sauce over the shrimp; cover with the Parmesan cheese and paprika. Bake for about 12 minutes, then serve.

168

SHRIMP WITH FRESH DILL

4 tablespoons butter or margarine
1 bunch green onions, chopped
2 tablespoons garlic, minced
2 lbs. raw shrimp, peeled and deveined
⅓ cup dry white wine
¼ cup fresh lemon juice
¼ teaspoon salt
¼ teaspoon white pepper
2 teaspoons fresh dill, finely chopped
1 tablespoon fresh parsley, finely chopped

Serves four

In a large skillet, melt the butter or margarine over medium heat. Sauté the green onions and garlic until soft. Add the shrimp, wine, lemon juice, salt, and pepper; cook over medium heat for about 8 minutes. Stir in the fresh dill and parsley. Serve over cooked brown rice.

SHRIMP MAMOU

½ cup (1 stick) butter or margarine
1 large onion, finely chopped
3 garlic cloves, minced
1 green pepper, finely chopped
1 teaspoon salt
½ teaspoon black pepper
4 dashes Tabasco®
29 oz. canned tomatoes, mashed
2 lbs. boiled shrimp, peeled and deveined

Serves four

In a large skillet, melt the butter or margarine over medium heat; add the onion, garlic, green pepper, salt, black pepper, Tabasco,® and tomatoes. Reduce heat to low and simmer for 15 minutes. Add the shrimp and cook for about 3 additional minutes. Serve over cooked brown rice.

169

SHRIMP SCAMPI

2 tablespoons olive oil

2 tablespoons butter or margarine, melted

¼ cup fresh lemon juice

½ teaspoon black pepper

3 tablespoons green onion, finely chopped

4 garlic cloves, minced

2 lbs. raw shrimp, shelled and deveined

2 tablespoons fresh parsley, finely chopped

Heat the broiler

Serves four

In a shallow baking dish, combine olive oil, melted butter or margarine, lemon juice, black pepper, green onion, and garlic. Add the shrimp and coat thoroughly. Place the dish of shrimp in the broiler about 4 inches from the heat for about 2 minutes. Turn and broil on the other side for about 1 minute or until shrimp are pink and completely done. Arrange the shrimp on a serving platter and pour the remaining sauce over the shrimp. Sprinkle with parsley and serve.

RED PEPPER SHRIMP

½ cup olive oil

6 garlic cloves, minced

2 teaspoons crushed red pepper

2 lbs. raw shrimp, shelled and deveined

1½ cups dry white wine

1 cup green onion, finely chopped

1 teaspoon salt

Serves four

In a large skillet, heat the olive oil over medium heat. Add the garlic, crushed red pepper and cook for about 1 minute. Stir shrimp into garlic sauce and cook for about 2 minutes to coat with the sauce. Add the wine and cook for 4 to 5 minutes until shrimp turn pink. Stir in the green onion, salt, and sauté lightly; then serve.

GARLIC CHICKEN

3 lbs. chicken breast, boned, skinned and cut into 2 inch pieces

¾ lb. butter or margarine

5 garlic cloves, minced

4 green onions, finely chopped

1 tablespoon fresh parsley, finely chopped

3 teaspoons fresh dill, finely chopped

¾ teaspoon dried oregano

½ teaspoon salt

½ teaspoon black pepper

4 dashes Tabasco®

Preheat oven to 350° F.

Serves four

Place chicken in a baking dish. In a saucepan, melt the butter or margarine over low heat; add the garlic, green onions, parsley, dill, oregano, salt, pepper, Tabasco,® and cook for 2 minutes. Pour the mixture over the chicken. Bake for 25 minutes, turn chicken and bake for another 25 minutes. Turn oven to broil and place chicken under broiler for 4 minutes.

SIMPLE ROASTED CHICKEN

2 tablespoons olive oil

1 teaspoon paprika

1 teaspoon onion powder

3 teaspoons garlic powder

1 teaspoon salt

1 teaspoon black pepper

1 3 lbs. chicken

Preheat oven to 350° F.

Serves four

In a small bowl, combine all the ingredients, except for the chicken. In a roasting pan, place the chicken and completely coat with the seasoning mixture. Bake, covered, for ½ hour. Uncover and continue baking for another ½ hour, basting occasionally with pan juices, until the chicken skin is crispy.

ROMAN CHICKEN

1 cup olive oil

4 tablespoons fresh lemon juice

3 teaspoons dried oregano

2 teaspoons dried rosemary

2 teaspoons garlic powder

2 teaspoons fresh parsley, finely chopped

½ teaspoon salt

1 3 lbs. chicken, skinned and cut into pieces

Preheat oven to 350° F.

Serves four

In a medium-size bowl, combine all the ingredients, except for the chicken. Put the chicken in the bowl and completely coat with the seasoning mixture. Place the chicken on a baking sheet and cook for 1 hour.

PEASANT CHICKEN

2 tablespoons olive oil

2 lbs. boneless chicken breast

1½ cups onion, chopped

29 oz. canned tomatoes, drained and chopped

3 tablespoons tomato paste

2 tablespoons fresh parsley, chopped

3 teaspoons garlic powder

1½ teaspoons crushed red pepper

32 oz. cannellini beans, rinsed and drained

Serves four

In a large skillet, heat the olive oil over medium heat. Brown the chicken for 10 minutes on each side. Add the onion, sauté for 2 minutes, and drain excess liquid. In a bowl, combine the remaining ingredients and add to the chicken. Reduce the heat to low and simmer for 30 minutes.

CHICKEN PARADIS

1 3 lbs. chicken, cut into pieces
Stone ground whole wheat flour for dusting
3 tablespoons olive oil
¾ cup onion, finely chopped
3 cups fresh mushroom, sliced
2 cups chicken broth or stock (see Index)
¾ cup dry red wine
2 teaspoons salt
½ teaspoon black pepper
1 bay leaf
3 tablespoons fresh parsley, finely chopped

Serves four

Lightly dust the chicken with the flour. In a large skillet, heat the olive oil over medium-high heat. Cook the chicken for about 10 minutes turning occasionally to brown both sides. Place the chicken on a serving platter. Add the onion and mushrooms to the skillet and sauté for 5 to 6 minutes. Add the chicken broth or stock and red wine to the mixture. Stir in the salt, pepper, bay leaf, parsley, and mix well. Return the chicken to the skillet, cover, and simmer for 40 to 45 minutes.

CHICKEN TARA

1	4 lbs. chicken, cut into pieces

Stone ground whole wheat flour for dusting

4 tablespoons butter or margarine

3 tablespoons olive oil

1 cup onion, chopped

31 oz. canned black-eyed peas, undrained

¾ cup chicken broth or stock (see Index)

½ teaspoon dried oregano

¼ teaspoon salt

¼ teaspoon black pepper

¼ teaspoon paprika

3 dashes Tabasco®

1 large tomato, finely chopped

Serves four to six

Lightly dust the chicken with the flour. In a large Dutch oven, heat the butter or margarine and olive oil; cook chicken over medium heat, turning, until golden brown. Place the chicken on a serving platter. Sauté the onion in the Dutch oven until tender. Add the remaining ingredients, except for the tomato, and bring to a boil. Add the chicken pieces to the Dutch oven, pressing the chicken onto the black-eyed peas, and sprinkle the tomato over the top. Cover and simmer for 40 to 45 minutes.

CHICKEN MADRID

¾ cup olive oil

4 lbs. boneless chicken breast

2 cups dry white wine

2 tablespoons fresh parsley, finely chopped

1 teaspoon dried tarragon

3 tablespoons garlic, minced

1 bay leaf

¼ teaspoon salt

¼ teaspoon black pepper

Serves four to six

In a large skillet, heat the olive oil. Sauté the chicken, turning, for about 6 minutes on each side until golden. Add all of the remaining ingredients and bring to a boil. Reduce the heat and simmer, covered, for about 40 to 45 minutes.

CHICKEN CALIENTE

58 oz. tomato sauce

1½ cups onion, finely chopped

3 tablespoons chili powder

1 teaspoon salt

1 teaspoon ginger

2 teaspoons orange zest, finely grated

1 teaspoon dried oregano

3 lbs. boneless chicken breast, cut into 1 inch pieces

32 oz. canned red kidney beans, rinsed and drained

4 teaspoons Tabasco®

Serves six

In a large saucepan, combine the tomato sauce, onion, chili powder, salt, ginger, orange zest, and oregano. Bring to a boil and add the chicken. Reduce the heat, stir, and cook until done. Add the kidney beans, and Tabasco,® stir gently, and cook another 8 to 10 minutes. Serve over cooked brown rice.

CHICKEN PROVENCE

3 tablespoons olive oil	
1 4 lbs. chicken, cut into pieces	
1 teaspoon salt	
1 teaspoon black pepper	
1 large green pepper, chopped	
1 large onion, finely chopped	
4 garlic cloves, minced	
10 oz. frozen peas	

Serves four

In a large skillet, heat the olive oil. Season the chicken with the salt, pepper, and brown in the skillet. Place the chicken on a serving platter. Add the green pepper, onion, and garlic to the skillet and cook for 6 minutes, stirring frequently. Return the chicken to the skillet, cover, and cook over medium-low heat for 1 hour, continuing to stir frequently. Gently stir in the peas and cook for another 8 to 10 minutes. Serve over cooked brown rice.

CHICKEN PECAN

2 cups pecans, finely ground	
1 cup freshly grated Parmesan cheese	
1 teaspoon garlic salt	
1 teaspoon black pepper	
1 teaspoon dried basil	
4 tablespoons fresh lime juice	
8 boneless chicken breasts, skinless and flattened	
4 tablespoons olive oil	

Serves six to eight

In a large shallow dish, combine pecans, Parmesan cheese, garlic salt, pepper, and basil. In another shallow dish, pour the lime juice; dip the chicken in the juice and coat with the pecan mixture. In a large skillet, heat the olive oil. Add the chicken; cook on each side until done and golden.

CHICKEN GORGONZOLA

8 boneless chicken breasts, skinless
¼ teaspoon salt
¼ teaspoon black pepper
3 tablespoons butter or margarine
2 tablespoons olive oil
¾ cup chicken broth or stock (see Index)
¼ cup heavy cream
⅓ cup Gorgonzola cheese, crumbled
¾ cup walnuts, chopped
2 tablespoons fresh basil, chopped

Serves six to eight

Season the chicken with salt and pepper. In a large skillet, melt butter or margarine with olive oil over medium heat. Add the chicken, turning from side to side, until done. Place the chicken on a serving platter. Add the broth or stock to the skillet and boil for 2 minutes. Add heavy cream, Gorgonzola, walnuts, and basil. Cook, stirring, until cheese is melted. Remove from heat and pour over the chicken.

TEX-MEX CHICKEN

1 lb. boneless chicken breast, skinless and cut into 1 inch pieces
2 tablespoons olive oil
15 oz. medium salsa
1 cup chicken broth or stock (see Index)
½ cup green pepper, chopped
¼ cup pitted black olives, sliced
2 cups cooked brown rice
¾ cup sharp Cheddar cheese, shredded

Serves four

In a large skillet, cook and stir chicken in hot olive oil over medium heat until done. Stir in the salsa, chicken broth or stock, green pepper, and olives. Bring to a boil. Stir in the brown rice. Remove from heat and sprinkle with Cheddar cheese. Cover and allow to stand for 10 minutes, then serve.

CHICKEN DIJON

4 boneless chicken breasts, skinless
2 tablespoons fresh lemon juice
2 tablespoons olive oil
2 green onions, thinly sliced
2 tablespoons fresh parsley, finely chopped
4 tablespoons Dijon mustard
1 tablespoon black pepper
½ teaspoon cayenne pepper
Heat the broiler
Preheat oven to 325° F.

Serves four

In a broiling pan, place the chicken breasts. In a medium-size bowl, combine the lemon juice, olive oil, green onions, parsley, mustard, and mix well. Spread the mixture over the chicken breasts. Broil 4 inches from the broiler for 10 minutes. Sprinkle both the black and cayenne peppers over the chicken and bake in the oven for 50 minutes.

CREAMY SHERRY CHICKEN

4 tablespoons butter or margarine

8 boneless chicken breasts, skinless

1 teaspoon salt

1 teaspoon black pepper

1 teaspoon nutmeg

1 lb. fresh mushrooms, sliced

¾ cup onion, finely chopped

½ cup fresh parsley, finely chopped

¼ cup fresh basil, finely chopped

1 cup dry sherry

2 teaspoons Dijon mustard

3 medium tomatoes, chopped

1½ cups half and half

Serves four to six

In a large skillet, melt the butter or margarine. Season the chicken breasts with the salt, pepper, and nutmeg. Place the chicken in a skillet and lightly brown. Add the mushrooms, onion, and sprinkle with the parsley and basil. Cook for 20 minutes, then reduce the heat. Stir in the sherry and mustard, cover, then simmer until the chicken is done. Remove the chicken from the skillet and place on a warm serving platter. Stir the tomatoes and half and half into the mixture remaining in the skillet. Reduce the mixture, stirring occasionally, until thickened, about 8 to 10 minutes. Pour sauce over the chicken and serve.

LITE CHICKEN

½ teaspoon ginger

1 teaspoon curry powder

¾ teaspoon crushed red pepper

3 tablespoons olive oil

2 lbs. boneless chicken breast, skinless

3 garlic cloves, minced

½ cup celery, sliced

½ cup red bell pepper, cut into strips

½ cup yellow bell pepper, cut into strips

½ cup dry white wine

½ cup chicken broth or stock (see Index)

3 tablespoons green onion, finely chopped

Serves four

In a bowl, combine ginger, curry powder, and crushed red pepper. Rub the mixture thoroughly onto the chicken. In a skillet, heat the olive oil and sauté the chicken. Remove the chicken and place on a serving platter. Sauté the garlic, celery, and peppers for about 2 minutes. Return the chicken to the skillet. Combine the wine and chicken broth or stock; add to the skillet. Reduce the mixture, stirring occasionally. Cook the chicken until done; then serve and garnish with green onion.

TURKEY WINGS CACCIATORE

4 turkey wings

1 teaspoon salt

1 teaspoon black pepper

1 cup onion, chopped

2 cups fresh mushrooms, sliced

2 garlic cloves, minced

2 medium green peppers, sliced

2 cups dry white wine

4 cups tomatoes, chopped

2 tablespoons fresh parsley, finely chopped

1 teaspoon dried oregano

Heat the broiler

Serves four

Split the wings at each joint and discard the tips. Broil the turkey wings, turning, until evenly browned. In a Dutch oven, combine all the remaining ingredients; add the wings. Cover and simmer over low heat, stirring occasionally, until turkey is tender. Uncover and cook another 20 minutes until sauce has thickened. Serve over cooked whole grain pasta.

CAJUN TURKEY BURGERS

1 lb. ground turkey

2 green onions, thinly sliced

1 red bell pepper, finely chopped

2 teaspoons garlic, minced

¾ teaspoon dried thyme

½ teaspoon ground cumin

½ teaspoon paprika

1 teaspoon crushed red pepper

4 dashes Tabasco®

Heat the broiler

Serves four

In a bowl, mix the turkey with the green onions, red bell pepper, garlic, thyme, cumin, paprika, crushed red pepper, and Tabasco.® Form the ground turkey mixture into 4 patties. Broil the turkey burgers 4 inches from the broiler, about 6 minutes per side or until done; then serve.

TURKEY SLOPPY JOES

3 tablespoons olive oil
1½ lbs. ground turkey
1½ cups onion, chopped
½ cup celery, chopped
¾ cup green pepper, chopped
3 garlic cloves, minced
8 oz. tomato sauce
⅓ cup Worcestershire sauce
¾ cup water
1 teaspoon salt
1 teaspoon black pepper
4 dashes Tabasco®

Serves four to six

In a large skillet, heat the olive oil and cook the turkey until brown. Add the onion, celery, green pepper, and garlic to the skillet; sauté until soft. Add the remaining ingredients and simmer for 30 to 45 minutes, then serve.

ITALIAN PORK CHOPS

3 tablespoons olive oil
4 8 oz. center cut pork chops
16 oz. canned tomatoes, mashed
¾ cup dry white wine
2 medium onions, finely chopped
1 tablespoon capers, drained
1 teaspoon garlic powder
¼ teaspoon dried thyme
½ teaspoon salt
½ teaspoon black pepper
4 dashes Tabasco®

Serves four

In a large skillet, heat the olive oil over medium-high heat and add the pork chops. Brown the chops about 3 minutes on each side, then turn off the heat. In a large bowl, combine the remaining ingredients and mix well. Pour the mixture over the pork chops; cover, and simmer over a low heat for 20 to 30 minutes or until the chops are tender.

FRENCH PORK CUTLETS

4 tablespoons mayonnaise (see Index)
3 tablespoons Dijon mustard
2 tablespoons fresh lemon juice
2 tablespoons dried dill
4 boneless pork loin cutlets, ¼ inch thick
2 tablespoons stone ground whole wheat flour
3 tablespoons butter or margarine

Serves four

In a small bowl, combine the mayonnaise, mustard, lemon juice, and dill. Dust the cutlets with the flour. In a large skillet, heat the butter or margarine and sauté the cutlets over medium-high heat. Reduce the heat to medium and brush the cutlets with the mayonnaise mixture. Cook the cutlets until tender, turning several times, while continuing to brush each cutlet with the mixture.

LEG OF LAMB

4 tablespoons olive oil
1 cup Worcestershire sauce
1 teaspoon salt
3 teaspoons black pepper
½ teaspoon ground thyme
1 teaspoon paprika
3 teaspoons garlic powder
1 8 lbs. leg of lamb
Preheat oven to 350° F.

Serves ten

In a small bowl, combine all of the ingredients, except for the lamb. Mix well, then coat all sides of the lamb with the mixture. Place the lamb in a roasting pan. Roast for 3 hours or until desired doneness and serve with the pan drippings.

GREEK LAMB BURGERS

2 lbs. ground lamb

½ teaspoon salt

½ teaspoon black pepper

2 teaspoons fresh rosemary, finely chopped

¼ teaspoon ground cumin

1 cup Feta cheese, crumbled

Heat the broiler

Serves four

In a bowl, combine the lamb with salt, pepper, rosemary, and cumin. Divide the lamb into 4 burgers. Place the burgers on a baking sheet and broil 3 inches under the broiler for 4 minutes. Turn the burgers and broil for an additional 3 minutes. Top each lamb burger with Feta cheese and broil for 1 more minute.

EASTER LEG OF LAMB

1 3 lbs. boneless leg of lamb

1 cup dry red wine

½ cup Italian salad dressing (see Index)

2 teaspoons dried rosemary

3 teaspoons garlic powder

1 teaspoon dry mustard

½ teaspoon salt

½ teaspoon black pepper

Preheat oven to 350° F.

Serves six

In a large baking dish, mix together all ingredients, except for the lamb. Place the lamb in the baking dish and marinate in the refrigerator, turning frequently, for 4 hours. Remove and discard marinade. Roast lamb, uncovered, for 2 hours or until done.

VEAL CHOPS DIJON

1 cup Dijon mustard
2 tablespoons whole black peppercorns, cracked
4 10 oz. veal chops
Heat the broiler
Serves four

In a small bowl, combine the mustard and pepper. Coat the veal chops completely with a thick coating of the mixture. Broil for 14 minutes or to desired doneness, turning the chops halfway through the broiling.

VEAL SCALLOPINI

2 lbs. veal cutlets, ¼ inch thick medallions
1 teaspoon salt
¼ teaspoon black pepper
1 cup Marsala wine
½ cup stone ground whole wheat flour
8 tablespoons butter or margarine
1 cup beef broth or stock (see Index)
1 tablespoon fresh lemon juice
1 teaspoon dried oregano
¾ lb. fresh mushrooms, sliced
16 oz canned tomatoes, drained
3 tablespoons fresh parsley, finely chopped
Serves four

Salt and pepper the veal medallions and place them in a shallow bowl. Pour the wine over the medallions, marinate covered, in the refrigerator for 1½ hours. Remove the veal, reserving the wine. Dredge the medallions in the flour. In a large skillet, heat the butter or margarine and brown the veal on both sides. Add the broth or stock, lemon juice, reserved wine, oregano, mushrooms, tomatoes, and parsley. Simmer for 15 minutes, stirring occasionally. Serve with cooked whole grain pasta.

SMOTHERED CHOPPED SIRLOIN

⅓ cup olive oil

4 large onions, cut into ¼ inch thick slices

2 lbs. ground sirloin

1 teaspoon salt

1 teaspoon ground black pepper

1 teaspoon garlic powder

Serves four

In a large skillet, heat the olive oil and sauté the onions for 25 minutes until caramelized and crisp. Remove onions and set aside. In a medium-size bowl, combine the ground sirloin, salt, pepper, and garlic powder; mix well and form into 4 chopped steaks. Cook the chopped steaks in the skillet over medium-high heat for 8 minutes, turning halfway through the cooking. Return the onions to the skillet for 2 to 3 minutes to reheat, then serve.

NUEVO LAREDO POT ROAST

1   4 lbs. rump roast

1 teaspoon salt

1 teaspoon black pepper

1½ cups onion, chopped

2 teaspoons garlic, minced

1 cup green pepper, chopped

1 cup beef broth or stock (see Index)

3 tablespoons chili powder

¼ teaspoon cayenne pepper

32 oz. canned red kidney beans, rinsed and drained

Preheat the oven to 400° F.

Serves eight

Season the roast with salt and pepper; place in a large roasting pan. Bake for 10 minutes, then turn the roast over and bake for another 10 minutes, to brown both sides. Add the onion, garlic, green pepper, beef broth or stock, chili powder, and cayenne. Spoon the sauce over the roast, cover, and continue baking for 2 hours, turning the roast every 30 minutes. Add the kidney beans and continue cooking until the roast is tender. Slice the roast and serve with the beans.

ROASTED BEEF TENDERLOIN

1 4 lbs. tenderloin of beef
5 garlic cloves, thinly sliced
3 tablespoons olive oil
3 tablespoons Worcestershire sauce
1 teaspoon salt
1 teaspoon ground black pepper
Preheat oven to 425° F.

Serves eight

Cut small, deep slits all over the meat and insert the sliced garlic in each of the slits. In a small bowl, mix the olive oil, Worcestershire, salt, and pepper. Rub the mixture over the tenderloin and place the meat in a shallow roasting pan; roast for 15 minutes. Reduce the temperature to 350° F. and roast for another 30 minutes for medium rare.

SIRLOIN STEAKS WITH ROSEMARY AND MUSHROOMS

2 tablespoons butter or margarine
2 tablespoons olive oil
4 12 oz. sirloin steaks
2 cups fresh mushrooms, sliced
½ cup green onion, sliced
1 tablespoon fresh rosemary, finely chopped
2 teaspoons garlic, minced
1 teaspoon black pepper
⅓ cup dry red wine

Serves four

In a large skillet, melt the butter or margarine and stir in the olive oil. Add the sirloins to the skillet and cook over medium heat to desired doneness. Place the sirloins on a serving platter, keeping them warm. Reserve the drippings and combine with the mushrooms, green onion, rosemary, garlic, and pepper; sauté while stirring over medium heat until the mushrooms are tender. Reduce the heat and add the wine, cooking until heated through. Spoon the mixture over the steaks and serve.

SIRLOIN STEAKS WITH ONIONS

4 12 oz. sirloin steaks

1 teaspoon ground black pepper

2 tablespoons butter or margarine

½ cup onion, finely chopped

⅓ cup beef broth or stock (see Index)

⅓ cup dry red wine

Serves four

Press pepper onto both sides of sirloins. In a large skillet, cook steaks in heated butter or margarine over medium heat to desired doneness. Transfer the steaks to a serving platter, reserving the drippings in the skillet while keeping the steaks warm. Stir the onions into the reserved drippings and sauté until the onion is tender. Add the broth or stock and wine to the onion mixture, stirring thoroughly. Bring to a boil, then reduce the heat. Cook at a low boil, uncovered, about 3 minutes until mixture is reduced to preferred consistency. Spoon over steaks and serve.

SOUTHWEST SIRLOIN STEAKS

1½ tablespoons chili powder

¾ teaspoon ground cumin

¾ teaspoon salt

½ teaspoon cayenne pepper

4 tablespoons butter or margarine

4 12 oz. sirloin steaks

15 oz. canned black beans, rinsed and drained

2 cups medium salsa

Serves four

In a small bowl, combine the chili powder, cumin, salt, and pepper. Press the mixture into the steaks on both sides evenly. In a large skillet, melt the butter and margarine, then cook the steaks to desired doneness. In a medium-size bowl, combine the beans and salsa until blended well. Pour the bean mixture over the steaks and simmer 5 to 10 minutes before serving.

BEEF TENDERLOIN AND MUSHROOM STEW

3 lbs. tenderloin tips, cut into pieces
¼ cup butter or margarine
1 tablespoon stone ground whole wheat flour
2 garlic cloves, minced
4 cups beef broth or stock (see Index)
1½ cups dry red wine
1 cup water
1 teaspoon black pepper
2 teaspoons salt
1½ cups fresh mushrooms, sliced
3 large onions, finely chopped
Preheat the oven to 325° F.

Serves six

In a large skillet, sauté the beef in the butter or margarine until browned. Stir in the flour and garlic, then transfer to a roasting pan. Combine the beef broth or stock, red wine, water, pepper, and salt; pour over the beef. Cover the roasting pan and bake for 2 hours. Add the mushrooms and onions to the roasting pan and return to the oven until tender. Serve over whole grain pasta or brown rice.

SPICY BEEF STEW

4 tablespoons olive oil

2 lbs. boneless stew beef

2 cups onion, chopped

2 cups green pepper, chopped

3 garlic cloves, minced

16 oz. tomato sauce

1 teaspoon salt

1 teaspoon black pepper

2 teaspoons hot chili powder

¼ teaspoon cayenne pepper

Serves four

In a large skillet, heat 3 tablespoons of the oil and brown the meat. Place the meat in a bowl and set aside. Add the remaining 1 tablespoon oil to the skillet and sauté the onion, green pepper, and garlic until tender. Return the meat to the skillet and add the remaining ingredients. Cover and simmer until done; then serve over cooked brown rice.

KENTUCKY BOURBON FILET MIGNON

2 tablespoons soy sauce

4 9 oz. filets mignon

2 tablespoons ground black pepper

⅔ cup bourbon

4 tablespoons Dijon mustard

½ cup heavy cream

2 tablespoons butter or margarine

Serves four

Rub the soy sauce on the filets. Press the pepper onto all sides of the meat. Marinate in the bourbon for 1 hour turning occasionally. In a large skillet, melt the butter or margarine and sauté the filets for 15 to 20 minutes or until desired doneness. Place the filets on a heated platter. Deglaze the skillet with bourbon. Quickly whisk in the mustard and cream, reduce the mixture, and pour over the filets before serving.

FILET MIGNON WITH GORGONZOLA AND PISTACHIO NUT SAUCE

4   9 oz. filets mignon

3 tablespoons olive oil

2 tablespoons butter or margarine

3 tablespoons green onion, finely chopped

¼ teaspoon salt

¼ teaspoon black pepper

3 tablespoons pistachio nuts, chopped

½ cup dry red wine

¼ cup beef broth or stock (see Index)

⅓ lb. Gorgonzola cheese, crumbled

Serves four

   In a large skillet, heat the olive oil and sauté the filets to desired doneness. Place on a serving platter and keep warm. Add to the skillet the butter or margarine, green onion, salt, pepper, nuts, red wine, and broth or stock; reduce the mixture. Remove from the heat and whisk in the cheese until melted. Return the mixture to the heat to thicken; then spoon over the filets and serve.

HERBED RIB EYE STEAKS

4   12 to14 oz. rib eye steaks

4 tablespoons butter or margarine

¾ cup green onion, chopped

2 teaspoons fresh basil, finely chopped

1 teaspoon salt

1 teaspoon black pepper

1 cup tomato, chopped

Serves four

   In a large skillet, melt the butter or margarine and cook the rib eyes to desired doneness. Place the steaks on a serving platter and keep warm. Reserve the drippings in the skillet. Sauté the green onion, basil, salt, and pepper in the reserved drippings until the onions are tender. Stir in the tomato and heat through. Spoon over the steaks and serve.

PASTA & PIZZA

SPANISH PASTA

¼ cup butter or margarine

1½ cups onion, chopped

8 oz. whole grain spaghetti, broken into large pieces

15 oz. beef broth or stock (see Index)

2 cups pitted green olives, drained and chopped

½ teaspoon black pepper

Serves four

In a large skillet, melt the butter or margarine, and sauté the onion, until soft. Add the pasta and cook for 10 minutes; then mix in the remaining ingredients. Reduce the heat to low; cover, simmer until the pasta is cooked and almost all of the liquid is absorbed.

SPICY MACARONI

1 lb. whole grain macaroni

¾ cup freshly grated Parmesan cheese

½ cup olive oil

14 oz. canned tomatoes, drained and chopped

1 teaspoon salt

½ teaspoon black pepper

½ teaspoon crushed red pepper

Serves four

In a large pot of boiling water, cook the macaroni; drain and put in a large bowl. Add ½ cup of the Parmesan cheese, olive oil, tomatoes, salt, black pepper, and crushed red pepper; toss to mix. Place in a serving bowl, sprinkle the remaining cheese over the pasta and serve.

GREEK PASTA

1 lb. ground lamb
1 cup onion, chopped
14 oz. canned tomatoes, undrained and chopped
6 oz. tomato juice
¾ cup beef broth or stock (see Index)
¼ teaspoon garlic powder
1 cup whole grain macaroni
1 cup frozen peas
1 cup frozen cut green beans
¾ cup Feta cheese, crumbled

Serves four

In a large skillet, cook the ground lamb and onion until the meat is brown; then drain. Add the undrained tomatoes, tomato juice, beef broth or stock, and garlic powder; bring to a boil. Stir in the macaroni, green peas, and green beans to the meat mixture; return to a boil. Reduce the heat, cover, and simmer until macaroni, peas, and green beans are tender. Sprinkle with the Feta cheese and serve.

PASTA WITH CHEESE AND HERBS

3 tablespoons butter or margarine
1 large onion, chopped
4 garlic cloves, minced
1 lb. whole grain macaroni
1½ cups sour cream
2½ cups Ricotta cheese
2 tablespoons fresh parsley, chopped
4 tablespoons fresh basil, chopped
2 tablespoons fresh oregano, chopped
¼ teaspoon salt
1 teaspoon black pepper
2 tablespoons freshly grated Parmesan cheese

Serves four

In a large skillet, melt the butter or margarine; sauté the onion and garlic until tender. Cook the pasta in boiling water. In a small bowl, mix the sour cream and Ricotta cheese to a smooth consistency. Add the parsley, basil, oregano, salt, and pepper; stir well. Combine this mixture with the sautéed onion and garlic, stirring frequently over a very low heat. When the pasta has cooked, drain and rinse well. Toss the pasta in a serving dish with the hot cheese sauce. Sprinkle with the Parmesan cheese and serve.

PASTA ROMANO

1 lb. whole grain pasta

5 tablespoons butter or margarine

⅓ cup olive oil

1 cup fresh basil, finely chopped

5 garlic cloves, minced

1 cup freshly grated Romano cheese

½ teaspoon salt

½ teaspoon black pepper

¼ teaspoon dried oregano

¼ teaspoon crushed red pepper

Serves four

In a large pot of boiling water, cook the pasta until tender, then drain. Keep the pasta warm in a large bowl. In a skillet, heat the butter or margarine and olive oil. Add the basil and garlic; sauté until tender. Add the remaining ingredients to the basil and garlic mixture. Toss the mixture with the pasta; then serve.

PASTA CHEDDAR

1 lb. whole grain pasta

1 cup sour cream

3 tablespoons fresh parsley, finely chopped

1 lb. sharp Cheddar cheese, finely grated

¼ teaspoon salt

1 teaspoon ground black pepper

Serves four

In a large pot of boiling water, cook the pasta until tender. Drain and put into a large bowl. Add the sour cream, parsley, Cheddar cheese, salt, pepper, and toss lightly to coat; then serve.

PASTA WITH THREE CHEESES

12 oz. whole grain shells
2 cups broccoli, steamed and chopped
1½ cups milk
4 oz. cream cheese, chopped
½ teaspoon ground black pepper
¾ cup Swiss cheese, shredded
¼ cup freshly grated Parmesan cheese

Serves four

In a large pot of boiling water, cook the pasta until tender. Drain and put into a large bowl. In a saucepan, combine the milk, cream cheese, and pepper. Cook and stir over low heat until the cheese has melted; add the pasta and the broccoli to the saucepan. Toss the pasta until it is completely coated with the mixture. Gently, stir in the Swiss and Parmesan cheeses. Place in a bowl and serve.

GARLIC PASTA

2 lbs. whole grain pasta
18 garlic cloves, minced
1½ cups olive oil
1 teaspoon crushed red pepper
½ teaspoon salt
1 teaspoon dried thyme
11 oz. chicken broth or stock (see Index)

Serves eight

In a large pot of boiling water, cook the pasta until tender. Drain and put into a large bowl. In a saucepan, cook the garlic in the oil until tender; stir in the pepper, salt, and thyme. Gradually, add the chicken broth or stock and simmer until heated through. Toss with the pasta and serve.

EGGPLANT AND PASTA

3 eggplant, peeled and sliced into strips

6 tablespoons olive oil

1 lb. whole grain macaroni

16 oz. canned tomatoes, chopped

2 tablespoons tomato paste

1 teaspoon dried oregano

2 garlic cloves, minced

salt and freshly ground black pepper to taste

½ cup water

8 oz. Mozzarella cheese, finely chopped

2 tablespoons butter or margarine

½ cup freshly grated Parmesan cheese

Preheat oven to 350° F.

Serves six

Lightly grease a casserole dish. In a large skillet, heat the oil, and brown the eggplant on both sides. Remove the eggplant and place on the side. In a large pot of boiling water, cook the pasta until tender; drain and put into a large bowl. In the skillet, place the pasta and add the tomatoes, tomato paste, oregano, and garlic. Mix well and season with the salt and pepper. Add a little of the water, if necessary, to moisten the mixture. Place the eggplant, Mozzarella, and pasta mixture in alternate layers in the casserole dish; continue until all the ingredients are used. Dab the butter or margarine over the top layer; sprinkle with the Parmesan cheese, and bake uncovered for about 30 minutes, until the top is bubbling and golden brown.

PASTA WITH PORCINI MUSHROOMS

2 oz. dried porcini mushrooms
1 tablespoon olive oil
1 cup onion, chopped
½ cup prosciutto ham, chopped
1 cup peas
½ cup sun-dried tomatoes, chopped
4 garlic cloves, minced
1 lb. whole grain spaghetti
⅓ cup freshly grated Parmesan cheese
½ cup fresh parsley, chopped

Serves four

Soak porcini mushrooms for 1 hour, then dry. In a large skillet, heat the olive oil and sauté the onion, prosciutto, peas, mushrooms, tomatoes, and garlic until tender. In a large pot of boiling water, cook the pasta until tender. Drain and put into a large bowl. Toss the pasta thoroughly with the sauce from the skillet; then toss with the cheese and parsley before serving.

FETTUCCINE WITH CREAM, HAM AND PEAS

4 tablespoons butter or margarine
1½ cups heavy cream
1 cup frozen peas
½ lb. ham, chopped
¾ cup freshly grated Parmesan cheese
1 lb. whole grain fettuccine

Serves four to six

In a large skillet, melt the butter or margarine; add the cream and bring to a boil. Cook for about 3 minutes to thicken then add the peas and ham; cook for an additional 2 minutes. Remove from the heat and stir in 2 table-spoons of the Parmesan cheese. In a large pot of boiling water, cook the pasta until tender. Drain and put into a large bowl. Pour the pasta into the skillet with the cream sauce and toss. Sprinkle with the remaining Parmesan cheese and serve.

201

FETTUCCINE WITH SPINACH AND CREAM

2 tablespoons butter or margarine

3 tablespoons onion, finely chopped

1½ cups heavy cream

1 cup fresh spinach, stems removed

1 teaspoon salt

¼ teaspoon black pepper

1 lb. whole grain fettuccine

3½ tablespoons fresh basil, chopped

1 cup freshly grated Parmesan cheese

Serves four to six

In a large saucepan, melt the butter or margarine; sauté the onion and cook until tender. Add the cream and bring to a boil, cooking for about 3 minutes to thicken the sauce. Add the spinach and sauté until wilted. Season with the salt and pepper; then remove from heat. In a large pot of boiling water, cook the pasta until tender. Drain and put into a large bowl. Pour the cream sauce into a bowl with the pasta. Add the basil and toss together. Sprinkle with the Parmesan cheese and serve.

MEATLESS LASAGNA

4 tablespoons olive oil
3 garlic cloves, minced
1 medium onion, chopped
2 stalks celery, chopped
32 oz. canned tomatoes, chopped
1 small can tomato paste
8 tablespoons tomato juice
¼ teaspoon salt
¼ teaspoon black pepper
15 sheets whole grain lasagna noodles
2 cups Mozzarella cheese, finely chopped
Preheat oven to 350° F.

Serves six

Lightly grease a deep casserole dish. In a saucepan, heat the olive oil; sauté the garlic and onion until tender. Add the celery, tomatoes, tomato paste, tomato juice, salt, and pepper. Stir well, cover, and simmer for about 45 minutes. In a large pot of boiling water, cook the lasagna noodles until tender; then drain. In the casserole dish, layer the noodles, sauce, and Mozzarella. Repeat these layers until all the ingredients are used. Top the dish with a layer of the cheese and bake for 30 minutes. Cut and serve immediately.

FRESH SPINACH AND RICOTTA LASAGNA

15 oz. Ricotta cheese
3 cups fresh spinach, chopped
1 cup fresh basil, finely chopped
1½ cups crushed red pepper
4 cups pasta sauce
1 cup water
½ lb. whole grain lasagna noodles
1 lb. Mozzarella cheese, finely chopped
1½ cups freshly grated Parmesan cheese
Preheat oven to 350° F.

Serves four

In a bowl, combine the Ricotta, spinach, basil, and crushed red pepper. In a 13 inch x 9 inch baking pan, mix 1 cup of the pasta sauce and ½ cup of the water; spread over the bottom of the pan. Completely cover the bottom of the pan with lasagna noodles. Top with ½ of the Ricotta mixture, 1 cup pasta sauce, ½ of the Mozzarella and sprinkle with ½ of the Parmesan cheese. Cover with another layer of noodles. Top with the remaining Ricotta mixture, 2 cups pasta sauce and ½ cup water. Top with the remaining Mozzarella and Parmesan cheeses. Cover with aluminum foil and bake for 30 minutes. Uncover and bake for 25 minutes, until the cheese is bubbling.

PASTA PRIMAVERA

1 lb. cooked whole grain pasta

4 tablespoons olive oil

2 tablespoons butter or margarine

6 garlic cloves, minced

½ lb. asparagus, chopped

2 zucchini, thinly sliced

½ cup peas

1 cup broccoli, chopped

1 cup cauliflower, chopped

1 medium onion, sliced

3 teaspoons basil, finely chopped

1 cup chicken breast, cooked and chopped (optional)

1 cup chicken broth or stock (see Index)

10 fresh mushrooms, sliced

1 lb. Rigatoni cheese, grated

Serves six

In a large skillet melt the butter or margarine with the olive oil; then sauté the garlic, vegetables, and basil until almost tender. Add the chicken, chicken broth or stock, and mushrooms. Bring to a boil; reduce heat, cover, and simmer for 5 minutes, stirring well. Toss with the cooked whole grain pasta; then sprinkle with the Rigatoni cheese before serving.

PASTA NAPOLI

2 lbs. cooked whole grain spaghetti
2 chickens, skinless and cut into pieces
2 large onions, sliced
2 teaspoons garlic, minced
90 oz. canned tomatoes, mashed
2 teaspoons fresh basil, finely chopped
½ teaspoon salt
3 teaspoons ground black pepper
1 cup freshly grated Parmesan cheese
Preheat oven to 375° F.

Serves eight

In a casserole dish, place the chicken; top with the onion and garlic. Cover with the mashed tomatoes and sprinkle with the basil, salt, and pepper. Bake in the oven for 1 hour and 20 minutes. Serve over the spaghetti and top with the Parmesan cheese.

LINGUINE WITH CHICKEN AND PEPPERS

3 cups chicken breast, cooked and sliced

1 lb. cooked whole grain linguine

4 tablespoons olive oil

4 garlic cloves, minced

2 cups green pepper, chopped

1½ cups heavy cream

3 tablespoons tomato paste

2 tablespoons fresh parsley, chopped

2 tablespoons crushed red pepper

Serves four

In a large skillet, heat the oil and sauté the garlic and onion until tender. Stir in the green pepper and add the cream, tomato paste, parsley, and crushed red pepper. Cook until the sauce thickens, add the chicken, and simmer until heated through. Toss with the linguine; then serve.

LINGUINE WITH TURKEY

1 lb. cooked whole grain linguine
3 tablespoons olive oil
2 large onions, chopped
6 garlic cloves, minced
1½ lbs. ground turkey
2 cups water
3 cups tomatoes, chopped
12 oz. tomato paste
1 teaspoon dried oregano
½ teaspoon salt
½ teaspoon black pepper
⅓ cup freshly grated Parmesan cheese
2 tablespoons fresh parsley, chopped

Serves six

In a large pot, heat the olive oil; sauté the onions and garlic until tender. Add the ground turkey, and cook for 5 minutes until the turkey is brown. Add the water, tomatoes, tomato paste, oregano, salt, and pepper, mixing well. Reduce the heat to low and simmer for 1½ hours, stirring occasionally. Place the linguine on a serving platter and top with the sauce. Sprinkle with the Parmesan cheese and parsley before serving.

CRABMEAT STROGANOFF

1 lb. cooked whole grain noodles

2 tablespoons butter or margarine

6 oz. fresh mushrooms, sliced

¼ cup dry white wine

½ teaspoon thyme

1 teaspoon salt

1 teaspoon black pepper

¾ lb. lump crabmeat

1½ cups sour cream

Serves four

In a large skillet, melt the butter or margarine and sauté the mushrooms, wine, thyme, salt, and pepper until the mushrooms are tender; bring the mixture to a boil. Reduce the heat to low and simmer for 10 minutes, stirring occasionally. Gently, add the crabmeat and warm in the mixture. Remove from the heat and stir in the sour cream. Toss with the pasta and serve.

PASTA CAPRI

1 lb. cooked whole grain cappelini

⅔ cup olive oil

1 lb. raw large shrimp, peeled and deveined

½ cup tomatoes, chopped

4 garlic cloves, minced

2 tablespoons fresh basil, chopped

½ teaspoon salt

½ teaspoon crushed red pepper

½ teaspoon black pepper

⅓ cup freshly grated Parmesan cheese

Serves six

In a large skillet, heat the oil. Add the shrimp, tomatoes, garlic, basil, salt, red and black peppers. Cook for 4 minutes or until done, turning the shrimp to cook on all sides. Add the shrimp mixture to the cappelini. Sprinkle with the Parmesan cheese, toss well, and serve.

Pizza

PIZZA CRUST

2 cups stone ground whole wheat pastry flour
¼ teaspoon Ki-Sweet or ½ teaspoon granulated Sweet 'N Low®
1 teaspoon salt
1 teaspoon butter or margarine
1 cup milk
½ teaspoon yeast
Preheat oven to 400° F.

In a bowl, place all the ingredients except the yeast. Mix all the ingredients together until smooth. Add the yeast and knead. Make a ball out of the dough and put in a greased bowl. Place in the refrigerator for about 20 to 30 minutes. Roll out the dough on a floured surface. Place the dough on a pizza pan. Cover with your favorite pizza topping and bake for 15 to 20 minutes.

TEDITO'S PIZZA MARGHERITA

15 oz. canned tomatoes, drained and chopped

1 tablespoon fresh basil, chopped

½ teaspoon dried oregano

½ teaspoon garlic powder

½ teaspoon salt

½ teaspoon ground black pepper

7 oz. Mozzarella cheese, thinly sliced

2 tablespoons olive oil

1 prepared stone ground whole wheat pizza crust (see Index)

Preheat oven to 400° F.

Serves four

In a small bowl, combine all the topping ingredients, except the Mozzarella cheese and the olive oil. Spread the mixture evenly over the pizza dough, then top with the Mozzarella slices. Bake in the oven for 15 to 20 minutes and drizzle with the olive oil before serving.

FRESH TOMATO PIZZA WITH PESTO

½ cup pesto

3 medium tomatoes, thinly sliced

½ teaspoon ground black pepper

¾ cup pitted black olives, sliced

2 cups Mozzarella cheese, shredded

1 prepared stone ground whole wheat pizza crust (see Index)

Preheat oven to 400° F.

Serves four

Spread the pesto evenly over the pizza dough. Arrange the tomato slices on top and season with the pepper. Sprinkle with the olives and Mozzarella cheese; bake for 15 to 20 minutes before serving.

FRESH HERB PIZZA

4 tablespoons olive oil

1 tablespoon fresh rosemary, finely chopped

1 tablespoon fresh marjoram, finely chopped

1 tablespoon green onion, finely chopped

1 tablespoon fresh basil, finely chopped

1 tablespoon fresh parsley, finely chopped

1 tablespoon onion, chopped

2 teaspoons garlic, minced

¼ teaspoon salt

¼ teaspoon black pepper

1 prepared stone ground whole wheat pizza crust

Preheat oven to 400° F.

Serves four

Spread the olive oil over the pizza dough; then sprinkle the dough evenly with the rosemary, marjoram, green onion, basil, parsley, onion, garlic, salt, and pepper. Bake in the oven for 15 to 20 minutes, then serve.

CLASSIC ITALIAN PIZZA

2 tablespoons butter or margarine, melted
6 garlic cloves, minced
½ teaspoon salt
¼ cup freshly grated Parmesan cheese
1 cup Mozzarella cheese, shredded
1 tablespoon fresh parsley, chopped
1 prepared stone ground whole wheat pizza crust
Preheat oven to 400° F.

Serves four

In a small bowl, combine the butter or margarine, garlic, and salt; mix well. Brush the mixture evenly over the dough; top with the cheeses and parsley. Bake for 15 to 20 minutes, then serve.

FOUR CHEESE PIZZA

2 oz. Gorgonzola cheese, thinly sliced
2 oz. Brie cheese, thinly sliced
2 oz. Fontina cheese, thinly sliced
2 oz. Mozzarella cheese, thinly sliced
2 tablespoons olive oil
1 prepared stone ground whole wheat pizza crust
Preheat oven to 400° F.

Serves four

Top the pizza dough with the four cheeses. Bake for 15 to 20 minutes, sprinkle with the olive oil, and serve.

GORGONZOLA AND WALNUT PIZZA

4 tablespoons olive oil
10 oz. Gorgonzola cheese, sliced
⅔ cup walnuts, chopped
½ teaspoon ground black pepper
1 prepared stone ground whole wheat pizza crust
Preheat oven to 400° F.

Serves four

Drizzle the pizza dough with the olive oil. Top the dough with the Gorgonzola and the walnuts; sprinkle with the pepper. Bake for 15 to 20 minutes, then serve.

THE LITTLE LADY PIZZA

1 cup Ricotta cheese
6 garlic cloves, minced
1 cup Mozzarella cheese, shredded
⅓ cup freshly grated Parmesan cheese
½ teaspoon Italian seasoning
¼ teaspoon onion powder
¼ teaspoon salt
1 tablespoon fresh parsley, chopped
1 prepared stone ground whole wheat pizza crust
Preheat oven to 400° F.

Serves four

In a bowl, combine all the ingredients, except the parsley and mix well. Spread the mixture over the pizza dough. Sprinkle with the parsley and bake for 15 to 20 minutes, then serve.

PIZZA SYRACUSA

1 cup pasta or pizza sauce

6 oz. fresh spinach, chopped

2 cups tomato, chopped

1½ cups cucumber, peeled and chopped

½ cup pitted black olives, drained and sliced

1 cup Feta cheese, crumbled

1 teaspoon salt

¾ cup Mozzarella cheese, shredded

1 prepared stone ground whole wheat pizza crust

Preheat oven to 400° F.

Serves four

Spread the pasta or pizza sauce evenly over the dough. Top with the remaining ingredients and bake for 15 to 20 minutes; then serve.

FRESH SPINACH AND PECAN PIZZA

1 tablespoon olive oil
½ cup onion, chopped
3 garlic cloves, minced
4 cups fresh spinach, chopped
½ teaspoon crushed red pepper
1 cup Swiss cheese, shredded
¼ cup pecans, chopped
1 cup Colby cheese, shredded
1 prepared stone ground whole wheat pizza crust
Preheat oven to 400° F.

Serves four

In a skillet, warm the oil; sauté the onion and garlic until tender. Add the spinach and crushed red pepper; cover, and cook for 2 minutes. Sprinkle the Swiss cheese over the dough; top with the spinach mixture. Sprinkle with the pecans and Colby cheese over the top of the pizza and bake for 15 to 20 minutes.

FRESH MUSHROOM PIZZA

2 tablespoons olive oil
5 cups fresh mushrooms, sliced
1 teaspoon garlic powder
½ teaspoon salt
½ cup pasta or pizza sauce
1 cup Mozzarella cheese, shredded
1 teaspoon crushed red pepper
1 prepared stone ground whole wheat pizza crust
Preheat oven to 400° F.

Serves four

In a large skillet, heat the olive oil and sauté the mushrooms until tender. Drain and stir in the garlic powder and salt. Spread the pasta or pizza sauce and then the mushrooms evenly over the top of the pizza dough. Sprinkle with the cheese and crushed red pepper; then bake for 15 to 20 minutes.

FRESH VEGETABLE PIZZA

2 cups olive oil

1 cup fresh mushrooms, sliced

½ cup broccoli, chopped

½ cup green pepper, chopped

½ cup onion, chopped

½ teaspoon garlic powder

¼ teaspoon dried oregano

1 cup pasta or pizza sauce

½ cup pitted black olives, drained and sliced

1 cup tomato, chopped

1 cup Mozzarella cheese, shredded

⅓ cup freshly grated Parmesan cheese

1 prepared stone ground whole wheat pizza crust

Preheat oven to 400° F.

Serves four

In a skillet, heat the olive oil and sauté the mushrooms, broccoli, green pepper, onion, garlic powder, and oregano for about 5 minutes; then drain. Spread the pasta or pizza sauce evenly over the pizza dough and top with the vegetable mixture. Sprinkle with the olives and tomato; then top with the cheeses and bake for 15 to 20 minutes.

219

ASPARAGUS AND HAM PIZZA

1½ cups cooked asparagus tips

1 cup ham, chopped

6 oz. Mozzarella cheese, sliced

4 tablespoons olive oil

¼ teaspoon ground black pepper

6 tablespoons freshly grated Parmesan cheese

1 prepared stone ground whole wheat pizza crust

Preheat oven to 400° F.

Serves four

Arrange the asparagus, ham, and Mozzarella cheese on top of the pizza dough. Drizzle with the olive oil and sprinkle with the pepper. Top with the Parmesan cheese and bake for 15 to 20 minutes.

HAM AND SWISS PIZZA

3 tablespoons olive oil

¾ cup green pepper, chopped

½ cup onion, chopped

1 tablespoon Dijon mustard

½ teaspoon crushed red pepper

1 cup ham, chopped

1 cup tomato, chopped

1 cup Swiss cheese, shredded

1 prepared stone ground whole wheat pizza crust

Preheat oven to 400° F.

Serves four

In a large skillet, heat the oil; cook the green pepper and onion until tender. Stir in the mustard and crushed red pepper, then set aside. Top the dough with the pepper-onion mixture, ham, and tomatoes. Sprinkle with Swiss cheese and bake for 15 to 20 minutes.

FAT HARRY'S PIZZA

¼ cup butter or margarine, melted
⅓ cup hot pepper sauce
2 cups cooked chicken, diced
½ cup celery chopped
4 oz. Roquefort cheese, crumbled
1 prepared stone ground whole wheat pizza crust
Preheat oven to 400° F.

Serves four

In a bowl, combine the butter and hot pepper sauce; mix well. Add the chicken and celery; toss to coat. Spread evenly over the pizza dough; then sprinkle with the Roquefort cheese and bake for 15 to 20 minutes.

NEAPOLITAN PIZZA

8 oz. Mozzarella cheese, thinly sliced
4 anchovy fillets in oil, drained and cut in half
4 medium tomatoes, chopped
1 tablespoon dried oregano
¼ teaspoon salt
½ teaspoon ground black pepper
4 tablespoons olive oil
1 prepared stone ground whole wheat pizza crust
Preheat oven to 400° F.

Serves four

Cover the pizza dough with the Mozzarella cheese. Top with the anchovies and then with the tomatoes. Sprinkle the oregano, salt, and pepper over the dough. Drizzle the olive oil evenly over the top and bake for 15 to 20 minutes.

THE TEXAS DEPUTY DOG PIZZA

½ lb. ground beef
2 tablespoons hot chili powder
½ cup onion, chopped
16 oz. hot salsa, well drained
1 cup Monterey Jack cheese, shredded
½ cup pitted black olives, drained and sliced
1½ cups sharp Cheddar cheese, shredded
1 cup shredded iceberg lettuce
1½ cups tomato, chopped
1 prepared stone ground whole wheat pizza crust
Preheat oven to 400° F.

Serves four

In a skillet, brown the ground meat for about 7 minutes and drain. Reduce the heat to low; add the chili powder and onion. Simmer for 2 minutes, stirring occasionally. Remove from the heat. Spread the salsa over the pizza dough; top with the Monterey Jack cheese, the beef mixture, olives, and Cheddar cheese. Bake for 15 to 20 minutes; top with the lettuce and tomato, then serve.

SMOKED SALMON AND BRIE PIZZA

12 oz. Brie cheese, sliced
8 oz. smoked salmon, thinly sliced
½ cup onion, chopped
2 oz. red caviar
1 prepared stone ground whole wheat pizza crust
Preheat oven to 400° F.

Serves four

Top the dough with the Brie cheese, smoked salmon, and onion. Bake for 15 to 20 minutes; spread with the caviar and serve.

SIDE DISHES OR
VEGETARIAN'S FARE

BROCCOLI ROMANO

3 tablespoons olive oil

2 garlic cloves, minced

½ teaspoon salt

½ teaspoon black pepper

20 oz. frozen broccoli spears, room temperature

½ cup freshly grated Romano cheese

Serves four

In a large skillet, heat the olive oil; sauté the garlic, salt, pepper, and broccoli until tender. Place the broccoli in a serving dish and sprinkle with the Romano cheese.

SAUTEÉD BROCCOLI

1 lb. broccoli florets, chopped and cooked

2 tablespoons olive oil

¼ cup Italian bread crumbs (see Index)

¼ cup freshly grated Parmesan cheese

¼ teaspoon salt

¼ teaspoon black pepper

1 teaspoon fresh basil, chopped

Serves four

In a saucepan, heat the olive oil and sauté the broccoli for 3 minutes. Add the bread crumbs, cheese, salt, and pepper. Toss and sprinkle with fresh basil.

FRIED CABBAGE

⅓ lb. raw bacon, chopped

1 head cabbage, shredded

1 medium onion, chopped

¼ teaspoon salt

¼ teaspoon black pepper

½ teaspoon garlic powder

Serves four

In a large skillet, cook the bacon until crisp. Add the cabbage, onion, salt, pepper, and garlic powder. Cover and cook on medium-low heat about 30 minutes until the cabbage is tender.

HONG KONG CABBAGE

¼ cup butter or margarine

4 cups cabbage, chopped

1 cup onion, chopped

1 cup celery, chopped

1 medium green pepper, chopped

½ teaspoon salt

½ teaspoon black pepper

2 tablespoons soy sauce

¼ teaspoon paprika

Serves four to six

In a skillet, melt the butter or margarine; add the remaining ingredients and sauté for 3 minutes. Cover and simmer until tender.

CAULIFLOWER AND TOMATOES

1 medium head cauliflower, chopped and cooked

1 tablespoon butter or margarine

½ cup onion, thinly sliced

2 large tomatoes, finely chopped

¼ teaspoon garlic powder

¼ teaspoon salt

¼ teaspoon black pepper

1 tablespoon fresh parsley, chopped

Serves six

Place the cauliflower in a serving bowl. In a skillet, melt the butter or margarine and sauté the onion until tender. Add the chopped tomatoes with the remaining ingredients and heat well. Pour over the cauliflower and serve.

EGGPLANT AND ZUCCHINI CASSEROLE

1 large eggplant, peeled, cubed, and cooked

4 tablespoons butter or margarine

2 medium onions, chopped

2 garlic cloves, minced

1 lb. fresh mushrooms, sliced

6 zucchini, sliced

16 oz. canned tomatoes, chopped

¼ teaspoon salt

¼ teaspoon black pepper

1 teaspoon fresh oregano, chopped

1 tablespoon bread crumbs (see Index)

4 tablespoons freshly grated Parmesan cheese

Preheat oven to 350° F.

Serves four to six

In a skillet, melt the butter or margarine; sauté the onion and garlic until tender. Add the mushrooms, zucchini, and eggplant and continue to cook for 10 minutes stirring frequently. In a small saucepan, mix together the tomatoes, salt, pepper, and oregano; simmer gently for 10 minutes. Into a greased casserole dish, spoon some of the tomato mixture; then place on top a layer of the eggplant and mushroom mixture, followed by another layer of tomato mixture. Repeat until both mixtures are eliminated. Sprinkle the top with Parmesan cheese and bread crumbs. Cover and bake for 40 minutes. Remove the cover for the last 10 minutes to brown the topping.

GREEN BEANS WITH FRESH DILL

2 lbs. fresh green beans, cut and cooked

2 tablespoons butter or margarine

½ cup onion, finely chopped

1 cup heavy cream

2 teaspoons fresh dill, chopped

½ teaspoon fresh lemon juice

½ teaspoon salt

½ teaspoon black pepper

Serves six to eight

Place the green beans into a serving dish. In a skillet, heat the butter or margarine and sauté the onion until tender. Stir in the cream, fresh dill, lemon juice, salt, and pepper. Simmer slowly until sauce begins to thicken. Spoon the sauce over the green beans and serve.

GREEN BEANS AND MUSHROOMS WITH SOUR CREAM

1 lb. fresh green beans, cut and cooked

½ cup butter or margarine

1 cup onion, thinly sliced

1 lb. fresh mushrooms, sliced

1 cup sour cream

2 teaspoons paprika

1 teaspoon salt

½ teaspoon black pepper

Serves four

Place the green beans in a serving dish. In a large skillet, melt the butter or margarine and sauté the onion about 6 or 7 minutes. Add the mushrooms and continue to cook until tender. Reduce the heat to low; add the remaining ingredients mixing thoroughly. Pour the sauce over the green beans and serve.

RED PEPPER GREEN BEANS

1 lb. fresh green beans, cut and cooked

1 cup butter or margarine

2 cups onion, chopped

2 teaspoons crushed red pepper

¼ teaspoon salt

Serves four

In a large skillet, melt the butter or margarine; sauté the onion until tender adding the crushed red pepper and salt while the onion simmers. Add the green beans to the skillet and coat well with the red pepper mixture. Simmer for about 10 to 12 minutes and serve.

ONIONS AU GRATIN

3 tablespoons butter or margarine

8 cups onion, chopped

8 oz. sharp Cheddar cheese, shredded

8 oz. Monterey Jack cheese, shredded

½ teaspoon salt

½ teaspoon black pepper

1 tablespoon jalapeno peppers, chopped

Preheat oven to 350° F.

Serves eight

In a large skillet, melt the butter or margarine and sauté the onions about 10 minutes. In a medium-size bowl, combine 4 oz. of the Cheddar cheese, 4 oz. of the Monterey Jack cheese, salt, black pepper, jalapeno peppers, and cooked onions; mix well. Pour into a greased casserole dish. Combine the remaining cheeses; sprinkle over the onion mixture and bake for 30 minutes.

CREAMED PEAS

6 tablespoons butter or margarine

6 green onions, chopped

4 stalks celery, chopped

1 lb. fresh peas, cooked

¾ cup heavy cream

2 tablespoons fresh tarragon, finely chopped

½ teaspoon salt

½ teaspoon black pepper

Serves four

In a skillet, melt the butter or margarine; sauté the green onions and celery until tender. Add the peas and stir in the cream and tarragon. Cook for 5 minutes uncovered; add salt and pepper, then serve.

PEAS AND MUSHROOMS

4 tablespoons butter or margarine

2 cups fresh mushrooms, chopped

1 lb. fresh peas, cooked

1 cup sour cream

½ teaspoon salt

½ teaspoon black pepper

Serves four

In a skillet, heat the butter or margarine; sauté the mushrooms until tender. Stir in the peas and heat. Add the sour cream, salt, and pepper. Simmer briefly, then serve.

SQUASH AU GRATIN

2 lbs. yellow squash, peeled, cooked, and cut into pieces

½ cup onion, chopped

2 eggs

2 tablespoons butter or margarine, softened

½ teaspoon salt

¼ teaspoon black pepper

⅛ teaspoon cayenne pepper

¼ teaspoon paprika

1 cup sharp Cheddar cheese, shredded

Preheat oven to 350° F.

Serves eight

In a small skillet, sauté the onion until tender. In a large bowl, beat the eggs, butter or margarine, salt, peppers, and paprika together; add the squash and onion. Pour into a greased casserole dish. Sprinkle the cheese over the top and bake uncovered for about 30 minutes.

SPAGHETTI SQUASH VENEZIA

2 small spaghetti squash

1 cup Mozzarella cheese, chopped

2 cups tomatoes, chopped

½ cup green onion, sliced

½ cup pecans, chopped

¼ cup fresh parsley, chopped

2 tablespoons olive oil

2 garlic cloves, minced

½ teaspoon salt

½ teaspoon black pepper

2 tablespoons freshly grated Parmesan cheese

Preheat oven to 350° F.

Serves four

Halve the squash lengthwise and remove the seeds. Prick the skin all over the squash. Place in a baking dish, cut side down. Cover and bake for 1 hour or until tender. Using a fork, separate the squash pulp into strands. Leave the strands in the squash shell. Sprinkle ¼ of the Mozzarella cheese in each shell. Toss and press the mixture up the sides of the shell. In a bowl, combine the tomatoes, green onion, pecans, parsley, oil, garlic, salt and pepper. Spoon ¼ of the tomato mixture into each of the shells. Sprinkle with the Parmesan cheese; return to the baking dish. Place in the oven and bake uncovered for about 20 to 25 minutes.

SPICY CREAMED SPINACH

2 tablespoons butter or margarine

20 oz. frozen spinach, thawed and drained

1½ cups sour cream

1 teaspoon onion powder

½ teaspoon nutmeg

1 teaspoon salt

1 teaspoon black pepper

4 dashes Tabasco®

Serves four

In a large saucepan, melt the butter or margarine; add the spinach, stir, and heat. In a bowl, combine the remaining ingredients and stir in the spinach. Cook for about 3 minutes until well blended.

SPINACH AU GRATIN

20 oz. frozen spinach, cooked, and drained

3 eggs

1½ cups sharp Cheddar cheese, grated

1½ cups Swiss cheese, grated

¼ cup butter or margarine, melted

¼ teaspoon black pepper

Preheat oven to 350° F.

Serves four

In a bowl, beat the eggs and mix in the cheeses, butter or margarine, salt, and pepper. Add the spinach to the egg mixture and stir. Pour into a greased casserole dish; cover and bake about 1 hour.

ZUCCHINI WITH FRESH MINT

3 tablespoons olive oil

7 cups zucchini, sliced

2 teaspoons fresh mint, chopped

2 teaspoons garlic, minced

½ teaspoon Dijon mustard

1 teaspoon salt

½ teaspoon black pepper

Serves four to six

In a large skillet, heat the oil and add the remaining ingredients. Stir and sauté for 15 to 20 minutes.

ZUCCHINI AND TOMATOES

3 tablespoons olive oil

3 cups tomatoes, chopped

2 garlic cloves, minced

½ teaspoon dried thyme

½ teaspoon dried basil

2 tablespoons fresh parsley, finely chopped

1 teaspoon salt

1 teaspoon black pepper

4 cups zucchini, chopped

Serves four

In a large skillet, heat the oil. Add the remaining ingredients, except the zucchini. Cover and cook for 6 minutes. Add the zucchini; cover and cook for 15 minutes, stirring well.

LENTILS WITH CURRY

2 tablespoons olive oil

2 medium onions, chopped

3 garlic cloves, minced

2 tablespoons curry powder

1 teaspoon ground cumin

1½ cups lentils, washed and drained

3 cups water

2 tablespoons fresh lemon juice

½ teaspoon lemon zest, finely grated

½ teaspoon salt

½ teaspoon black pepper

Serves four

In a large saucepan, heat the oil and sauté the onion until tender. Add the garlic, curry powder, and cumin. Cook for 2 minutes. Add the lentils and cook for about 3 minutes. Pour the water into the pan; add the lemon juice and zest. Bring to a boil; then add the salt and pepper. Cover; reduce the heat and simmer about 25 minutes stirring well, until lentils are done.

LIMA BEANS SEVILLE

30 oz. frozen lima beans, cooked and drained

2 tablespoons olive oil

1 cup onion, chopped

4 tablespoons medium salsa

½ teaspoon salt

½ teaspoon black pepper

Serves six

In a saucepan, heat the oil and sauté the onion until tender. Reduce the heat and add the remaining ingredients. Cook for about 10 minutes, stirring well.

WILD RICE AND PEAS

4 tablespoons butter or margarine

8 green onions, thinly sliced

½ cup wild rice, washed and drained

½ cup brown rice, washed and drained

2 cups water

1 cup peas

¼ teaspoon salt

½ teaspoon black pepper

Serves four

In a saucepan, heat the butter or margarine and sauté the green onions. Stir the wild rice and brown rice into the mixture. Add the water and stir over a high heat. Add the peas, salt, and pepper. Stir well, cover, and leave over a low heat until all liquid has been absorbed.

OKRA AND BROWN RICE

30 oz. frozen cut okra, cooked and drained

1 cup cooked brown rice (see Index)

2 tablespoons butter or margarine

1 cup onion, chopped

½ teaspoon garlic powder

1 teaspoon Tabasco®

½ teaspoon salt

Serves six to eight

In a skillet, melt the butter or margarine; add the onion, garlic powder, Tabasco,® and salt; sauté until tender. Add the okra; cook about 2 minutes. Mix in the rice and simmer for about 5 minutes.

BROWN RICE PRIMAVERA

3 cups cooked brown rice (see Index)
1 tablespoon olive oil
1 garlic clove, minced
2 cups broccoli, chopped
1 cup zucchini, sliced
1 cup fresh mushrooms, sliced
1 medium tomato, chopped
¼ cup fresh parsley, chopped
⅓ cup mayonnaise (see Index)
½ cup milk
¼ cup freshly grated Parmesan cheese
½ teaspoon black pepper

Serves six

In a large skillet, heat the oil and sauté the garlic, broccoli, zucchini, and mushrooms until tender. Add the tomato and parsley; cook for about 2 minutes. Remove the vegetables and set aside. To the same skillet, add the mayonnaise, milk, cheese, and pepper; cook, stirring until smooth. Add the brown rice and mix well. Return the vegetables to the skillet; heat and serve.

HERBED STOVE TOP BROWN RICE

1 cup brown rice

3 tablespoons butter or margarine

½ cup onion, chopped

½ cup green pepper, chopped

2 garlic cloves, minced

¼ teaspoon salt

½ teaspoon black pepper

2 cups chicken broth or stock (see Index)

2 tablespoons fresh parsley, chopped

Serves four

In a saucepan, mix together all the ingredients, except for the parsley. Cover and bring the mixture to a boil, stirring occasionally. Lower the heat and simmer for about 45 minutes or until the liquid is absorbed; stir in the parsley before serving.

BROWN RICE AU GRATIN

1½ cups onion, chopped
2 tablespoons butter or margarine
2 cups cooked brown rice
2 eggs, beaten
1 cup milk
1 cup Swiss cheese, shredded
1 teaspoon salt
½ teaspoon white pepper
¼ teaspoon paprika
½ cup freshly grated Parmesan cheese
2 teaspoons fresh parsley, chopped
Preheat oven to 375° F.

Serves four

In a skillet, melt the butter or margarine and sauté the onion until softened. In a bowl, mix all the ingredients, except for the paprika, Parmesan cheese, and parsley. Into a greased baking dish, pour the mixture and top with the parsley, Parmesan cheese, and paprika. Bake for 25 to 30 minutes.

COOKED BROWN RICE

1 cup brown rice
2¼ cups water
salt and black pepper to taste

Serves four

Place the rice in a saucepan and add 2¼ cups of water. Bring the mixture to a boil over high heat. Stir the rice, then reduce the heat to low and cover the pan. Simmer for 30 to 40 minutes, remove the pan from the heat and let the rice sit, covered, for a few minutes in the pan. Just before serving, fluff the rice with a fork and season with salt and pepper.

CRÈME FRAICHE SWEET POTATOES

4 large sweet potatoes, unpeeled
½ cup crème fraiche
6 tablespoons cooked bacon, crumbled

Serves eight to ten

In a pot, boil the unpeeled sweet potatoes; then slice. Top each slice with a spoonful of the crème fraiche; then top with the crumbled bacon.

ITALIAN SWEET POTATOES

½ cup olive oil
2 teaspoons dried basil
1½ teaspoons dried oregano
2 teaspoons garlic powder
1 teaspoon salt
4 medium sweet potatoes, peeled and cubed
2 tablespoons fresh lemon juice
2 teaspoons fresh parsley, chopped
Preheat oven to 400° F.

Serves four to six

In a baking pan, combine the oil, basil, oregano, garlic powder, and salt; place in the oven for 5 minutes. Add the potatoes and toss to coat with the herb mixture. Bake for 45 minutes, turning until the potatoes are cooked and crisp. Drizzle on the lemon juice and sprinkle with the parsley.

SWEET POTATO AND ONION SAUTÉ

4 large sweet potatoes, peeled, sliced, and boiled

¾ cup butter or margarine

1 medium onion, chopped

½ teaspoon salt

½ teaspoon black pepper

Serves six

In a skillet, melt the butter and sauté the onion until browned; add the salt and pepper. Add the cooked potatoes to the skillet and cook over medium-high heat until the sweet potatoes are browned, turning the sweet potatoes only once or twice.

BLUE CHEESE BAKED SWEET POTATOES

4 medium sweet potatoes, unpeeled and washed

4 tablespoons butter or margarine

4 tablespoons sour cream

8 tablespoons Blue cheese, crumbled

Preheat oven to 400° F.

Serves four

Place the sweet potatoes on a baking sheet and bake in the oven for about 45 minutes or until done. Pierce each sweet potato through its center with a fork to determine the doneness. With a knife, slit the tops of each sweet potato lengthwise. Mix into each sweet potato 1 tablespoon butter or margarine, 1 tablespoon sour cream, and 2 tablespoons Blue cheese.

JUST MORE DESSERTS

BRIGITTA'S COFFEE ICE

4 cups cold drip coffee

3 teaspoons Ki-Sweet or 6 teaspoons granulated Sweet 'N Low®

whipping cream for garnish

In a metal bowl, mix the cold coffee and sugar substitute; place in the freezer. About every 30 minutes, remove the bowl from the freezer and stir to prevent the coffee from solidifying. Garnish with a dollop of whipped cream.

COFFEE PUNCH

1 gallon whole milk

16 oz. cold drip coffee

1 pint vanilla ice cream (see Index)

sugar substitute to taste

whipping cream for topping

chocolate (60% to 70% cocoa content), finely grated

In a large punch bowl, combine the coffee and milk. Add scoops of the vanilla ice cream and sugar substitute to taste. Serve in parfait glasses topped with whipped cream and sprinkles of chocolate.

PURPLE COW

1 scoop vanilla ice cream (see Index)

1 can diet coke

Combine in a large glass and enjoy.

PROFITEROLES

½ cup (1 stick) butter or margarine
pinch of salt
¼ teaspoon Ki-Sweet or ½ teaspoon granulated Sweet 'N Low®
1 cup water
1 cup stone ground whole wheat pastry flour
1 teaspoon vanilla extract
4 eggs
1 tablespoon lemon zest, finely grated
vanilla ice cream recipe (see Index)
chocolate sauce recipe (see Index)
Preheat oven to 400° F.

In a large saucepan, combine the butter or margarine, salt, sugar substitute, and water. Bring to a boil and cook until the butter or margarine is melted. Remove the saucepan from the heat; add the vanilla and flour. With a wooden spoon, beat until the mixture forms a ball that pulls away from the side of the pan. Add the eggs, one at a time, beating the mixture smooth after each egg; then add the lemon zest. Line a baking sheet with parchment paper and drop the mixture by the teaspoon onto the sheet. Bake for 10 minutes; then reduce the heat to 375° F. and bake for another 10 minutes. Let cool; then fill with vanilla ice cream and top with chocolate sauce.

VANILLA ICE CREAM

6 eggs

2 12 oz. cans evaporated milk

¼ teaspoon salt

1 tablespoon plus 2 teaspoons vanilla extract

2 teaspoons Ki-Sweet or 4 teaspoons granulated Sweet 'N Low®

3 tablespoons sugar-free syrup

1 cup whipping cream

Serves six

In a bowl, beat the eggs, evaporated milk, salt, and vanilla extract. Pour the mixture in a sauce pan and heat on a low-medium fire, until the sides of the pan begin to coat with the mixture or the mixture begins to bubble. Pour the mixture in the ice cream maker and add the whipping cream to the mixture. The ice cream should take approximately 30 minutes to 1 hour depending on the temperature of the mixture and your machine. Once the ice cream begins to harden add the syrup and the sugar substitute. Let the ice cream finish processing. Serve immediately or freeze for another time.

Optional: For coconut flavored ice cream, coconut extract can be substituted for the vanilla extract.

NEW ORLEANS STYLE BEIGNETS

½ cup (1 stick) butter or margarine
pinch of salt
¼ teaspoon Ki-Sweet or ½ teaspoon granulated Sweet 'N Low®
1 cup water
¼ teaspoon almond extract
1 teaspoon vanilla extract
1 cup stone ground whole wheat pastry flour
4 eggs
vanilla sauce recipe (see Index)
chocolate sauce recipe (see Index)
oil for deep frying
Heat oil in deep fryer to 350° F.

In a large saucepan, combine the butter or margarine, salt, sugar substitute, and water. Bring to a boil and cook until the butter or margarine is melted. Remove the saucepan from the heat. Add the almond extract and vanilla; then add the flour. Beat with a wooden spoon until the mixture forms a ball that pulls away from the side of the pan. Add the eggs to the dough, one at a time, beating the mixture smooth after each egg. Drop the dough by heaping teaspoons into the heated oil. Fry the beignets for 10 to 12 minutes; then turn them and fry until golden brown. Drain on paper towel. Spoon the vanilla sauce on each plate; place a beignet in the sauce and top with the chocolate sauce.

CHOCOLATE SAUCE

¾ cup heavy cream
¼ teaspoon Ki-Sweet or ½ teaspoon granulated Sweet 'N Low®
3½ oz. chocolate (60% to 70% cocoa content), finely chopped

In a saucepan, bring the cream and sugar substitute to a boil. Remove from the heat. Add the chocolate to the cream. After 1 minute, begin stirring from the center until the chocolate is completely dissolved.

CHOCOLATE CAKE WITH VANILLA SAUCE

7½ oz. chocolate (60% to 70% cocoa content), finely chopped
11 tablespoons unsalted butter or margarine
4 large eggs, separated
2 teaspoons Ki-Sweet or 4 teaspoons granulated Sweet 'N Low®
1 teaspoon vanilla extract
⅓ cup stone ground whole wheat pastry flour
Preheat oven to 350° F.

In a double boiler, melt the chocolate and butter or margarine; remove from heat and cool. Beat the egg yolks; add the sugar substitute and vanilla, beating until mixture is pale yellow and thick. Fold in the chocolate mixture and slowly add the flour until just blended. In a separate bowl, beat the egg whites until soft peaks are formed. Fold in ½ of the egg whites into the chocolate mixture and then the remaining ½ of the egg whites. Pour the batter into a 10 inch greased cake pan and bake for 20 minutes. When the cake cools, serve with the vanilla sauce.

VANILLA SAUCE

2 egg yolks
2 teaspoons Ki-Sweet or 4 teaspoons granulated Sweet 'N Low®
2 cups milk
2 teaspoons vanilla extract

In a bowl, beat the egg yolks and sugar substitute. In a saucepan, scald the milk and gradually add to the egg yolk mixture. Return the mixture to the saucepan, and stir constantly on medium heat until sauce coats the back of the spoon. Strain the sauce before adding the vanilla; then serve.

ALMOND SPONGE CAKE WITH GANACHE ICING

½ cup heavy cream
1 cup stone ground whole wheat pastry flour
1½ teaspoons baking soda
pinch of salt
3 eggs
8 teaspoons Ki-Sweet or 12 teaspoons granulated Sweet 'N Low®
2 teaspoons vanilla extract
1 teaspoon almond extract
Preheat oven to 350° F.

In a saucepan, scald the cream and remove from the heat. Combine the flour, baking soda, and salt. In a bowl, beat the eggs with the sugar substitute until thick and pale yellow in color. Fold in the flour mixture until smooth; then add the warm cream and both extracts. Pour immediately into a greased 9 inch spring form pan and bake for 25 to 30 minutes. Cool; then remove from pan. Pour the Ganache icing on top of cake; cut and serve.

GANACHE ICING

1 cup heavy cream
½ teaspoon Ki-Sweet or 1 teaspoon granulated Sweet 'N Low®
8 oz. chocolate (60% to 70% cocoa content), finely chopped

In a saucepan, bring the cream and sugar substitute to a boil. Remove from the heat. Add the chocolate to the cream. After 1 minute, begin stirring from the center until the chocolate is completely dissolved.

LEMON CHEESE POCKETS

8 oz. cream cheese, room temperature

1½ teaspoons Ki-Sweet or 3 teaspoons granulated Sweet 'N Low®

1 teaspoon vanilla extract

1 teaspoon lemon zest, finely grated

sour cream stone ground whole wheat pastry recipe (see Index)

Preheat oven to 375° F.

Mix all the ingredients, except for the pastry recipe, until well blended and smooth. Roll the sour cream pastry dough into a rectangle. Cut into small squares and drop a dollop of the cream cheese mixture in the center of each square. Form pockets by folding each of the 4 corners of each of the squares toward the center. Bake for 20 minutes; then serve.

SOUR CREAM WHOLE WHEAT PASTRY

2 cups stone ground whole wheat pastry flour

⅛ teaspoon salt

8 oz. unsalted butter or margarine

½ cup sour cream

Preheat oven to 375° F.

In a bowl, blend the flour and the salt. Cut the butter with a blender until the mixture is even and the size of peas. Mix in the sour cream; then work the dough with hands until a ball forms. Cover dough with plastic wrap and refrigerate for 4 hours. If baking, roll the dough on a floured surface; then bake in a greased pie pan until light brown.

MINI PEANUT BUTTER CHOCOLATE PIES

1¼ cups stone ground whole wheat pastry flour	
pinch of salt	
2 teaspoons Ki-Sweet or 4 teaspoons granulated Sweet 'N Low®	
5 tablespoons cold butter or margarine	
1 large egg	
1 large egg yolk	

Topping:

½ cup cream	
1 teaspoon Ki-Sweet or 2 teaspoons granulated Sweet 'N Low®	
5 oz. chocolate (60% to 70% cocoa content), finely chopped	
10 heaping tablespoons sugar free, all natural peanut butter	
Preheat oven to 400° F.	

Combine the flour, salt, sugar substitute, and butter or margarine; blend until the butter or margarine is in small pieces. Add the egg and egg yolk; blend well. Place the dough on a floured surface. Knead the dough and form into a disk; refrigerate for 1 hour. Grease 3 inch tart tins with butter or margarine. Roll out the dough; cut into circles and press the circles individually into the tart tin. Prick the bottom of each circle. Refrigerate for 30 to 60 minutes; then bake for about 12 to 15 minutes.

For the topping, in a saucepan, bring the cream to a boil. Remove from the heat and pour over the chocolate. After 1 minute, add the sugar substitute and mix all the ingredients until well blended.

Place a large tablespoon of the peanut butter into each of the tart shells; then pour on the topping. Refrigerate for 15 to 25 minutes; then serve.

CHOCOLATE PEANUT BUTTER COOKIES

1 tablespoon butter or margarine, melted
1 egg beaten
½ cup heavy cream
4 teaspoons Ki-Sweet or 8 teaspoons granulated Sweet 'N Low®
1½ teaspoons baking soda
¾ cup stone ground whole wheat pastry flour
⅓ cup sugar free, all natural peanut butter
½ cup chocolate (60% to 70% cocoa content), finely chopped
1 teaspoon vanilla extract
Preheat oven to 325° F.

In a bowl, combine the butter, egg, cream, and sugar substitute; then add the baking soda, flour, peanut butter, chocolate, and vanilla until well blended. Onto a greased cookie sheet, drop the cookie dough by individual teaspoons. Bake for 10 to 12 minutes.

WHOLE WHEAT GINGER MUFFINS

2 cups stone ground whole wheat pastry flour
1 teaspoon baking soda
½ teaspoon salt
½ teaspoon Ki-Sweet or 1 teaspoon granulated Sweet 'N Low®
1 egg
½ teaspoon ginger
¼ cup butter or margarine, melted
1 cup buttermilk
1 teaspoon lemon extract
1 tablespoon lemon zest, finely grated
Preheat oven to 375° F.

In a large bowl, combine all the ingredients, except the butter or margarine, milk, lemon extract and zest; then add the butter or margarine, milk, lemon extract and zest to the mixture and blend well. Pour into a greased muffin tin and bake for 17 minutes.

ALMOND TRUFFLES

½ cup heavy cream

8 oz. chocolate (60% to 70% cocoa content), finely chopped

1 cup almonds, chopped

In a saucepan, bring the cream to a boil. Remove from the heat and pour over the chocolate. After 1 minute, stir until well blended. Pour the mixture into a glass 9 x 9 inch dish; allow to cool to room temperature. Chill for several hours. When set, scoop with a mellon scooper into roughly shaped balls. Roll each ball into the chopped almonds. Place the balls on a baking sheet lined with parchment paper. Cover and refrigerate until serving.

ALANA BANANA CREAM PUDDING

3 tablespoons stone ground whole wheat pastry flour

¼ teaspoon salt

4 egg yolks

2 teaspoons Ki-Sweet or 4 teaspoons granulated Sweet 'N Low®

2 cups milk

1 teaspoon vanilla extract

1 teaspoon banana extract

1½ tablespoons butter or margarine, melted

In a bowl, combine the flour, salt, egg yolks, and sugar substitute. In a saucepan, scald the milk; then slowly add to the flour mixture. Return the mixture to the pot and cook over moderate heat until thickened, stirring constantly. Remove from the heat and return to the bowl. Stir in the vanilla and banana extracts. Spread the melted butter or margarine over a piece of saran wrap; lay the buttered side of the saran wrap directly on top of the mixture to prevent a skin from forming. Keep the bowl covered and chill.

ALMOND PASTRY CREAM

2 tablespoons stone ground whole wheat pastry flour
2 oz. ground almonds
pinch of salt
2 egg yolks
1 teaspoon Ki-Sweet or 2 teaspoons granulated Sweet 'N Low®
1 cup milk
½ teaspoon vanilla extract
½ teaspoon almond extract
1½ tablespoons butter or margarine, melted

In a bowl, combine the flour, almonds, salt, egg yolks, and sugar substitute. In a saucepan, scald the milk; then slowly add to the flour mixture. Return the mixture to the pot and cook over moderate heat until thickened, stirring constantly. Remove from the heat and return to the bowl. Stir in the vanilla and almond extracts. Spread the melted butter or margarine over a piece of saran wrap; lay the buttered side of the saran wrap directly on top of the mixture to prevent a skin from forming. Keep the bowl covered and chill.

CHOCOLATE MINT SOUFFLÉ

4 oz. chocolate (60% to 70% cocoa content), chopped

3 egg yolks

1 teaspoon mint extract

2 teaspoons Ki-Sweet or 4 teaspoons granulated Sweet 'N Low®

5 egg whites

Preheat oven to 400° F.

In a double boiler, melt the chocolate; remove from the heat. In a bowl, beat the egg yolks with the mint extract and blend well. Add the chocolate to the yolk mixture. In a separate bowl, beat the egg whites with the sugar substitute until stiff. Whisk ¼ of the egg whites into the chocolate mixture until well blended; then gently fold in the remaining egg whites. Pour the mixture into a greased 1 quart soufflé dish or into 4 to 6 greased ramekins and bake for 15 minutes.

BREADS AND
BREAD CRUMBS

STONE GROUND WHOLE WHEAT BREAD

2 cups hot milk
1½ teaspoons salt
1 package dry yeast
¼ cup warm water
4⅓ cups stone ground whole wheat pastry flour
Preheat oven to 375° F.

In a bowl, mix the milk and salt; let cool. Sprinkle the yeast over the warm water; allow to stand for 5 minutes. Add the yeast mixture to the bowl; then add the flour. Beat well and cover. Let rise in a warm place until doubles in size; then beat lightly. Pour into a loaf pan; cover and let rise again. Bake for 45 minutes.

BLUE CHEESE BREAD

2 packages dry yeast

2 cups warm water

2 tablespoons butter or margarine

⅓ cup freshly grated Parmesan cheese

¾ cup Blue cheese, crumbled and room temperature

2 teaspoons salt

4¼ cups stone ground whole wheat pastry flour

Preheat oven to 350° F.

Sprinkle the yeast over the warm water; allow to stand for 5 minutes. In a bowl, with an electric mixer, combine the butter or margarine, the Parmesan cheese, ½ cup of the Blue cheese, salt, and 3 cups of the flour for 2 to 3 minutes. Add in the remaining 1¼ cups flour with a spoon. Cover and allow to rise for about 45 minutes. Place the mixture into a well greased 2 quart casserole dish or pan. Spread the top with the remaining ¼ cup Blue cheese and bake for 30 to 55 minutes.

EASY PARMESAN BREAD

2 packages dry yeast
2 cups warm water
2 tablespoons butter or margarine
¾ cup freshly grated Parmesan cheese, plus 2 tablespoons
1 tablespoon thyme
1 tablespoon oregano
2 teaspoons salt
4¼ cups stone ground whole wheat pastry flour
Preheat oven to 350° F.

Sprinkle the yeast over the warm water; allow to stand for 5 minutes. In a bowl, with an electric mixer, combine the butter or margarine, ¾ cup Parmesan cheese, thyme, oregano, salt, and 3 of the cups of flour for 2 to 3 minutes. Add the remaining 1¼ cups flour with a spoon. Cover and allow to rise for about 45 minutes. Place the mixture into a well greased 2 quart casserole dish or pan. Sprinkle the top with the 2 tablespoons of Parmesan cheese and bake for 30 to 55 minutes.

STONE GROUND WHOLE WHEAT BISCUITS

1½ cups heavy whipping cream

2 cups stone ground whole wheat pastry flour

3 teaspoons baking powder

½ teaspoon salt

½ stick butter or margarine

Preheat oven to 450° F.

Whip the cream until firm or holds its shape. In a bowl, with an electric mixer, combine all the ingredients with the cream. Knead for 1 minute and roll out to about 1 inch thickness. Cut the biscuits with a cutter and place a pat of butter or margarine on the top of each biscuit. Bake for about 10 to 12 minutes.

CHEESE BISCUITS

1½ cups heavy whipping cream

2 cups stone ground whole wheat pastry flour

3 teaspoons baking powder

½ teaspoon salt

¼ cup Cheddar cheese, grated

¼ cup freshly grated Parmesan cheese

Preheat oven to 450° F.

Whip the cream until firm or holds its shape. In a bowl, with an electric mixer, combine all the ingredients with the cream. Knead for 1 minute and roll out to about 1 inch thickness. Cut the biscuits with a cutter and place a pat of butter or margarine on the top of each biscuit. Bake for about 10 to 12 minutes.

BREAD CRUMBS

1 box Triscuit®	
1 cup stone ground whole wheat flour	
2 tablespoons dried parsley flakes	

Yields 3 cups

Place Triscuit® in food processor and pulverize to crumbs. Add parsley and mix until well blended.

ITALIAN BREAD CRUMBS

1 box Triscuit®	
1 cup stone ground whole wheat flour	
½ cup grated Parmesan cheese	
2 tablespoons dried parsley flakes	
1 tablespoon Italian seasonings	
2 tablespoons garlic powder	

Yields 3½ cups

Place the Triscuit in a food processor and pulverize to crumbs. Add all other ingredients and mix until well blended.

RED WINES, WHITE WINES AND CHAMPAGNES

Compiled by wine expert and connoisseur, James C. Brennan and Brennan's Restaurant cellar master, Harry Hill.

Brennan's Restaurant of New Orleans continues to boast of its 35,000 bottle wine cellar with 3,000 different selections. In recognition of its excellence, Brennan's has received the Oscar of wine cellar awards, the *Wine Spectator Grand Award,* for seventeen consecutive years. The diverse composition of this outstanding cellar is largely attributable to the expertise and passion for wine of Jimmy Brennan, Ted Brennan's brother and a co-owner of Brennan's Restaurant. In the list that follows, Jimmy and Brennan's cellar master, Harry Hill, share their knowledge and understanding of red and white wines as well as champagne suggestions that are acceptable in moderation when you *SUGAR BUST FOR LIFE!...WITH THE BRENNANS.*

FRENCH RED WINES
Red Bordeaux

Chateau Beycheville
Chateau Calon-Segur
Chateau Canon
Chateau Cantemerle
Chateau Clos St. Anne, Gironde
Chateau Ducru Beaucaillou
Chateau Glaudet
Chateau Gloria
Chateau Grand Puy Lacoste
Chateau Haut-Batailley
Chateau Haut-Roucaud, Cotes-de-Castillion
Chateau Lapelletrie
Chateau Le Bon Pasteur
Chateau Talbot
Chateau Trimoulet

Red Burgundy

Aloxe-Corton, Domaine Reine Pedauque
Aloxe-Corton, Les Vercots, Tollot-Beaut and Fils
Beaune, Clos de la Mousse, Bouchard Pere and Fils
Bourgogne, Hautes Cotes du Nuits, Domaine Gros Frere et Soeur
Bourgogne, Reserve Du Domaine, Domaine Dominque Guyon
Chambertin, Domaine du Chateau de Beaune
Chambolle Musigny, Cave Privee, A Rodet
Chambolle Musigny, Domaine G. Roumier
Chambolle Musigny, Les Sentiers, Herve Sigavt
Chassagne-Montrachet, Clos de la Boudriotte, Vincent Girardin
Clos de la Roche, Joseph Drouhin
Corton, Clos du Roi, Prince Florent du Merode
Echezeaux, Joseph Drouhin
Gevrey-Chamberin, Vieille Vigner, Domaine Bachelet
Mercurey, Clos du Roi, Faiveley
Monthelie, Paul Garaudet
Nuits St. Georges, Les Boudots, A Gagey
Nuits St. Georges, Les Boudots, Domaine Jean Grivot
Pommard, Clos de la Platiere, Prince Florent de Merode
Pommard, Domaine Billard-Gonnet
Pommard, Jean Marc Boillot
Savigny-Les Beaune, La Dominode, Louis Jadot
Volnay, Caillerets, Ancienne Cuvee Carnot, Bouchard Pere et Fils
Volnay, Clos Des Angles, Olivier Leflaive
Vosne-Romanee, Domaine Jean Grivot
Vosne-Romanee, Gros Frere et Soeur
Vougeot, Les Cras, Mongeard-Mugneret

Rhone

Chateauneuf-du-Pape, Beaucastel
Chateauneuf-du-Pape, Chateau La Nerthe
Chateauneuf-du-Pape, La Bernardine, M. Chapoutier
Chateauneuf-du-Pape, La Crau, Domaine Vieux Telegraphe
Cotes du Rhone, E Guigal
Les Violettes, Cote du Rhone, Moillard
Saint Joseph, Le Grand Pompee, Paul Jaboulet Aine
Saint Joseph, Reserve Personelle, Paul Jaboulet Aine

French White Wines

Auxey-Duresses, Domaine du Duc de Magenta

Beaujolais Blanc Jadot, Le Bienvenues, Louis Jadot

Beaune, Clos des Mouches, Joseph Drouhin

Beaune, Les Greves Blanc, Louis Jadot

Bourgogne Chardonnay, La Vignee, Bouchard

Bourgogne Chardonnay, Laroche, Barrique Reserve

Bourgogne, Leroy

Chablis, Domaine de Vaudon, Joseph Drouhin

Chablis, Fourcharmes, Chateau De Maligny

Chablis, Grand Cru Moutonne, Long Depoquit Bichot

Chablis, Grand Cru Vaudesir, Domaine Moreau et Fils

Chablis, Grand Cru Vaudesir, Joseph Drouhin

Chablis, Grand Cru, Les Presuses, Jean Doubissat

Chablis, Les Vaillons, Vieilles Vignes, Domaine Laroche

Chablis, Saint Martin, Domaine Laroche

Chablis, Vaillons, Cuvee Prestige, Guy Moreau

Chassagne Montrachet, Laboure-Roi

Corton Charlemagne, J.M. Boillot

Corton Charlemagne, V. Girardin

Cotes De Nuits Villages

Meursault Charmes, G. Bocard

Meursault Charmes, Olivier Leflaive

Meursault, Bouchard Pere et Fils

Meursault, Les Perrieres, V Girardin

Meursault, Olivier Leflaive

Meursault, Reine Pedauque

Meursault, Vieille Vigne, Paul Garaudet

Pouilly Fuisse, Chateau Fuisse

Pouilly Fuisse, Chateau Fuisse, Les Combettes

Pouilly Fuisse, Chateau Fuisse, Vieilles Vignes

Pouilly Fuisse, Les Crays, Domaine Manciat-Poncet

Puligny Montrachet, Joseph Drouhin

Puligny Montrachet, Laboure-Roi

Puligny Montrachet, Les Champs Gains, Olivier Leflaive

Puligny Montrachet, Les Clavoillons, Domaine Gerard Chavy et Fils

Puligny Montrachet, Les Pucelles, J.M. Boillet

Puligny Montrachet, Les Pucelles, Olivier Laflaive

Puligny Montrachet, Rene Pedauque

Saint Aubin, 1er Cru En Remilly, Olivier Leflaive
Saint Aubin, 1er Cru Les Charmois, Domaine Bernard Morey
Saint Aubin, Louis Jadot
Saint Veran, Chateau Fuisse, J J Vincent
Savigny-Les-Beaune, Les Vermots Dessus, Domaine Vincent Gerardin
Savigny-Les-Beaune, Louis Jadot

Loire

Clos De La Bergerie, Chateau de la Roche-Aux-Moines, Nicholas Joly
La Doucette, Pouilly Fume
La Poussie, Sancerre
Vouvray, Chateau, Moncontour

Rhone

Chateauneuf-du-Pape, La Crau, Domaine Vieux Telegraph
Hermitage Blanc, Chante Alouette, M. Chapoutier
Hermitage Blanc, Chevalier de Sterimberg, P. Jaboulet
Saint Joseph, Deschants, M. Chapoutier

American Red Wines
Cabernet Sauvignon

Caymus, Napa
Corison, Napa
Delectus, Napa
Harrison Winery and Vineyard, Napa
Heitz Cellar, Napa
Lewis Cellars "L" Oakville Ranch, Napa
Lewis Cellars "L" Reserve, Napa
Oakford Vineyards, Oakville, Napa
Oakville Ranch, Napa
Pezzi King, Dry Creek, Sonoma
Silver Oak, Alexander, Sonoma
Silver Oak, Napa
The Terraces, Rutherford, Napa
Turnbull Wine Cellars, Oakville, Napa
Viader, Napa
Woodward Canyon, Washington

Merlot
Albini Family Vineyards, Russian River, Sonoma
Gary Farrell, Ladi's Vineyard, Sonoma
Gary Farrell, Russian River, Sonoma
Lewis Cellars, Oakville, Napa
Neyers Vineyard, Napa
Paradigm, Oakville, Napa
Pride Mountain, Napa
Selene, Napa
Swanson, Napa

Pinot Noir
Au Bon Climat, La Bauge, Bien Nacido Vineyard, Santa Barbara
Au Bon Climat, Mistral Vineyard, Central Coast
Babcock Vineyards, Santa Barbara
Babcock Vineyards, Santa Ynez Valley
Castalia, Russian River
Etude, Carneros
Fiddlehead Cellars, Oregon
Miner, Pisoni Vineyard, Monterey
Patz and Hall, Hyde Vineyard, Caneros and Russian River
Robert Mueller Cellars, Emily's Cuvee, Russian River
Rochioli, Russian River
Testarossa Vineyard, Santa Cruz Mountains
Williams Selyem, Russian River, Sonoma

Sangiovese
Benessere, St. Helena, Napa
Iron Horse, Alexander
Pietre Rosse, Dalla Valle Vineyards, Oakville, Napa
Venezia, Nuoyo Mondo Vineyard

Syrah
Foxen, Morehouse Vineyard, Santa Maria
McDowell Valley Vineyards, Mendocino
Unalii, Sonoma
Qupé, Santa Barbara

Zinfandel
A. Rafanelli Winery, Dry Creek, Sonoma
Gary Farrell, Sonoma
Hendry Ranch, Napa
Limerick Lane Cellars, Russian River, Sonoma
Nalle Winery, Dry Creek, Sonoma
Robert Biale Vineyards, Napa
Rosenblum Cellars, Alameda County
The Terraces, Rutherford, Napa

American Whites
Chardonnay
Arrowood, Sonoma
Beringer Reserve, Napa
Bernardus, Monterey
Bethel Heights Reserve, Oregon
Cakebread Cellars, Napa
Chateau Montelena, Napa
Chateau Potelle VGS, Napa
Chateau Potelle, Central Coast
Chateau St. Jean, Belle Terre Vineyard, Sonoma
Chateau St. Jean, Robert Young Vineyard, Sonoma
Chimney Rock, Carneros
Clos du Bois, Calcaire Vineyard
Clos Pegase, Mitsuko's Vineyard
Cuvaison, Carneros
Davis Bynum, Limited Edition, Russian River Valley
Davis Bynum, Russian River Valley
Deloach O.F.S., Russian River
Far Niente, Napa
Ferrari-Carano, Alexander
Ferrari-Carano Reserve, Alexander
Ferrari-Carano, Tre Monte, Alexander Valley
Ferrari-Carano, Tre Terre, Alexander Valley
Gary Farrell, Hedin Vineyard, Russian River
Gloria Ferrer, Carneros
Grgich Hills, Napa
Kistler, Sonoma

L'Ecole #41, Washington
Mac Rostie, Carneros
Mac Rostie Reserve, Carneros
Marimar Torres, Don Miguel Vineyard, Sonoma
Martin Ray, Mariage
Matanzas Creek, Sonoma
Mer Soleil, Central Coast
Miner Family, Napa
Mirassou Harvest Reserve, Monterey
Mondavi, Napa
Morgan, Monterey
Morgan Reserve, Monterey
Murphy Goode, Island Block, Reserve
Newton, Napa
Ovation, Joseph Phelps, Napa
Pine Ridge Dijon Clones, Carneros
Rochioli, Russian River
Rombauer, Napa
Rodney Strong, Chalk Hill Vineyard, Sonoma
Sanford Barrel Select, Santa Barbara
Shafer, Red Shoulder Ranch, Carneros
Silverado Limited Reserve
Sonoma Cutrer, Cutrer Vineyard, Russian River
Sonoma Cutrer, Les Pierres, Russian River
Sonoma Cutrer, Russian River
Stag's Leap Wine Cellars, Napa
Steele, California
Stuhlmuller Vineyard, Alexander
Swanson, Napa
Trefethen, Napa
Wild Horse, Central Coast

Sparkling Wines

Bollinger, Special Cuvee

Comte Audoin de Dampierre, Cuvee des Ambassadeurs, Brut

Comte Audoin de Dampierre, Brut Rose

Jean Milan, Blanc de Blanc, Brut Special

G.H. Mumm, Extra Dry, Champagne

Laurent Perrier, Brut

Perrier-Jouet, Extra Dry

Philipponnat, Grand Blanc

Pommery, Brut Royal

Pommery, Apanage, Brut Royal

Louis Roederer, Brut Premier

Ruinart, Brut

Taillevent, Brut

Taillevent, Grand Reserve Rose

Tattinger, La Francaise

Veuve Clicquot-Ponsardin, Champagne Brut, Yellow Label

Ca del Bosco, Franciacorta, Brut

Chandon, Brut, Napa

Chandon, Brut, Blanc de Noirs, Napa

Chandon, Cuvee 2000, Late Disgorged

Culbertson, Super Bowl XXIV, Commemorative

Gruet, Brut

Iron Horse, Wedding Cuvee, Sonoma

L'Ermitage, Brut, Anderson Valley

Mumm, Cuvee Napa, Blanc de Noirs

Mumm, Cuvee Napa, Brut Prestige

Roederer Estate, Brut, Anderson Valley

S. Anderson Brut, Napa Valley

Pacific Echo, Brut, Mendocino

Scharffenberger, Brut Rose, Mendocino

J. Schram, Napa Valley

Schramsberg, Blanc de Blanc, Napa

Michel Tribaut, Brut, Monterey County

"To Market, To Market!" Brand Name Guide

Learning to read a label is your only safeguard against ingredients in foods that appear to be healthy but actually are not. Reading the label creates an awareness of the large amount of sugar or other unhealthy ingredients that are in the foods we eat. Avoiding refined sugar and other high glycemic ingredients in food products is extremely difficult otherwise.

Fresh is best always. Frozen foods are a second choice. Canned foods, although many in our guide are not preserved in any type of sugar, should be the third choice.

Often people ask, "How many grams of sugar am I allowed per meal?" The answer is, "As few as possible." Remember that this is a *low sugar* dietary concept, not a *no sugar* dietary concept. There is natural sugar in fruit and vegetables as well as in the dairy products you are eating now.

There are few "rules" to follow. Knowing how to read a label, however, is a must. The amount of sugar per serving identified on the label of an acceptable food item should not exceed 1 gram. This means two things.

First, understand just how much a serving size is and only eat one or two servings. Second, if you dilute a serving size by adding another ingredient such as water, you may eat more than one or two servings depending upon the degree of dilution. As always, moderation is the key.

CAUTION! Inspection of a food product does not end at reading the number of sugar grams per serving. Reading the detailed list of ingredients is a must. This is where the "hidden sugars" and other unacceptable ingredients are found.

"Hidden Sugars" Include:

Beet Juice	High Fructose Corn Syrup
Beet Sugar	Honey
Brown Rice Syrup	Maltodextrin
Brown Sugar	Maltose
Cane Juice	Maple Syrup
Cane Syrup	Molasses
Corn Syrup	Raisin Juice
Dextrose	Sugar, Raw and Refined
Glucose	Sucrose

Other Unacceptable Ingredients Include:

Barley Malt

Cornstarch

Flour: Corn, Enriched Wheat and White

Malted Barley

Modified Food Starch

Modified Tapioca Starch

Potato Starch

Don't be confused! Fructose in fruit and lactose in milk are acceptable natural sugars. Interestingly, it is believed that maltodextrin, found in many "sugar free" products, has a glycemic index or response as high as refined sugar - a scary thought, in particular, for diabetics battling a life threatening disease. The Brennans recommend the use of maltodextrin very conservatively if at all. They chose sugar substitutes for their recipes and products for the brand name guide, which are void of maltodextrin.

The use of two new natural sugar substitutes is recommended. *Ki-Sweet* is the sweetener of choice by the Brennans in their dessert recipes. It is an all natural, low glycemic sweetener made from kiwi fruit and invented by Dr. Ann de Wees Allen, N.D. of the Glycemic Research Institute in Washington, D.C. You will appreciate how well it sweetens while cooking or baking.

Although not used in their recipes, the Brennans also suggest another new, natural sweetener, the herb *Stevia*. It is believed that both of these recommended new, natural sugar substitutes do not have the adverse side effects of many commonly used artificial sweeteners.

Most conventional artificial sweeteners such as aspartame, saccharin, acesulfame-K and sucralose as well as the sugar alcohols isomalt, maltitol, mannitol, sorbitol and xylitol are slowly absorbed inducing a low glycemic response. However, all are carbohydrates and should be used in moderation.

Variety in the usage of artificial sweeteners is an important consideration. Alternating the use of these various conventional sweeteners will reduce the ingestion of significant amounts of any one kind – thus diminishing the risk of potential side effects.

The Brennans understand that most people do not have the time required to avidly read labels in maintaining a truly healthful lifestyle; they have undertaken the challenge to help you. Originally, they compiled a list of acceptable brand names to choose. The Brennans have researched even more products and now offer an expanded Brand Name Guide. If a food item that you need is not recommended, check the recipe section for possible sugar free substitutions.

The guide predominantly notes brand names void of anything unacceptable. The Brennans recommend very few products containing even traces of "hidden sugars" and other unacceptable ingredients so as not to create confusion. However, ingredients listed in accordance with FDA guidelines at the bottom of a label can be insignificant.

Equally as insignificant can be small amounts of "forbidden" foods, "hidden sugars" or other unacceptable ingredients spread throughout large quantities of food. For example, the small amounts of Worcestershire sauce in some recipes should be inconsequential.

Beyond the Greater New Orleans area sugar free whole grain breads are limited and difficult to find. Homemade bread recipes provide a viable solution. Contacting the New Orleans bakery mentioned in the Brand Name Guide provides another option. As a third alternative, a store bought whole grain bread with minimal amounts of hidden sugar listed at the bottom of a label could be consumed in extreme moderation.

The extensive list of acceptable brand names is based on the inventories of over 25 grocery, health food and specialty stores in the New Orleans area, the Dallas-Fort Worth area, and the San Francisco/Monterey Bay areas. There is the possibility that certain appropriate brand names of which the Brennans are, simply, unaware have not been included. Occasionally, store shelves and freezers were incompletely stocked. In any event, the Brennans urge you to share the names of any additional items that may have been inadvertently excluded. They will include them in their next printing.

The updated brand name guide should expedite your grocery shopping and contribute to the ease of your low sugar lifestyle. Once again, the Brennans have taken the guesswork out of making wise choices. *SUGAR BUST FOR LIFE! ... WITH THE BRENNANS PART II* has revealed an easy road to a healthful life for you!

Anchovies
Haddon House Anchovy Fillets
Gourmet Award Anchovies
King Oscar Anchovies
Musette Anchovy Fillets
Reese Anchovies
Roland Anchovies
Giovanni Anchovy Paste
Reese Anchovy Paste
Roland Anchovy Paste

Baking Soda
Arm & Hammer Brand

Beans, Peas, Canned
Black Beans
Eden Organic Black Beans
Goya Black Beans
Green Giant Black Beans
Natural Value Organic Black Beans
Progresso Black Beans
Trappey's Black Beans
Westbrae Natural Black Beans
Whole Foods Black Beans
Black-Eyed Peas
Allen's Black-Eyed Peas
Blue Runner Black-Eyed Peas
Bush's Black-Eyed Peas
Goya Black-Eyed Peas
Green Giant Black-Eyed Peas
Shur Fine Black-Eyed Peas
Trappey's Black-Eyed Peas
Trappey's Black-Eyed Peas with
   Jalapenos
Butter Beans
Stubbs Butter Beans

Cannellini Beans
American Prairie Organic Cannellini
   Beans
DaVinci White Kidney Beans
Progresso White Kidney Beans
Whole Foods White Beans
Fava Beans
Progresso Fava Beans
Field Peas
Bush's Field Peas with Snaps
The Allens Sunshine Field Peas
Trappey's Field Peas
Garbanzo Beans/Chick Peas
Casa Fiesta Garbanzo Beans
Eden Garbanzo Beans
La Lechonera Chick Peas/Garbanzo
   Beans
Old El Paso Garbanzo Beans
Progresso Chick Peas/Garbanzo Beans
Westbrae Natural Garbanzo Beans
Whole Foods Garbanzo Beans
Great Northern Beans
Green Giant Great Northern Beans
Trappey's Great Northern Beans
Westbrae Natural Great Northern
   Beans
Green Beans
America's Choice Green Beans
Delchamps Green Beans
Del Monte Fresh Cut Green Beans
Del Monte Fresh Cut Seasoned Green
   Beans
Double Luck Green Beans
Food Club Green Beans
Good Day Green Beans
Green Giant Green Beans
Jack and the Bean Stalk Green Beans
Libby Green Beans
Le Sueur Green Beans
Pride Green Beans
Prestige Green Beans

Shur Fine Green Beans
S&W Cut Green Beans
The Allens Italian Green Beans
Thrifty Maid Green Beans

Lentils
Eden Organic Lentils
Eden Organic Lentils with Sweet Onion
  & Bay Leaf
Westbrae Natural Lentils
Whole Foods Lentils

Lima Beans
American Prairie Organic Baby Lima
  Beans
America's Choice Lima Beans
Thrifty Maid Lima Beans
Del Monte Fresh Cut Lima Beans
Trappey's Baby Green Lima Beans
Valu Time Lima Beans

Navy Beans
Eden Organic Navy Beans
Trappey's Navy Beans

Pinto Beans
Casa Fiesta Pinto Beans
Eden Pinto Beans
Old El Paso Pinto Beans
Progresso Pinto Beans
Trappey's Navy Pinto Beans
Westbrae Pinto Beans
Whole Foods Pinto Beans

Red Kidney Beans
DaVinci Red Kiney Beans
Eden Organic Chili Beans
Progresso Red Kidney Beans
Van Camp's New Orleans Style Red
  Kidney Beans
Westbrae Natural Chili Beans
Westbrae Natural Red Kidney Beans
Whole Foods Red Kidney Beans

Salad Beans
Westbrae Natural Salad Beans

Soy Beans
Eden Organic Black Soy Beans
Westbrae Natural Soy Beans

Soup Beans
Westbrae Natural Soup Beans

Wax Beans
America's Choice Cut Wax Beans
Del Monte Wax Beans
Shur Fine Wax Beans

Beans, Dried
All Brands

Beans, Refried
Bearitos (Vegetarian) Refried Beans -
  Spicy with Green Chilies
Mexicali Rose Refried Beans
Natural Value Organic Refried Black
  Beans
Natural Value Organic Refried Pinto
  Beans
Old El Paso Fat-Free Refried Beans
Old El Paso Refried Beans
Old El Paso Refried Black Beans
Ortega Refried Beans
Rosarita Refried Beans: Traditional,
  Spicy Jalapeno, Vegetarian & No-Fat
  Traditional
San Carlos Refried Beans
Shari's Organic Refried Black Beans
Shari's Organic Refried Pinto Beans
  with Roasted Garlic
Shari's Organic Refried Pinto Beans
  with Roasted Green Chile & Lime
Taco Bell Refried Beans

Beverages
Coffee
Diet Colas
Tazo-The Reincarnation of Tea
Any Brand Unsweetened Tea
Community Diet Iced Tea
After The Fall All Natural Diet Spritzers
R.W. Knudsen Spritzer, Flavored
R.W. Knudsen Thirst Quenchers

Snapple Diet Drinks - All Flavors

Sparkling Mineral Water: Plain & Flavored; Calistogo, Crystal Geyser, Perrier, San Pellegrino

Bread

Brother Juniper's Dark Rye (Pumpernickel)

Finn Crisp Thin Crisp Rye Bread

French Meadow Salt-Free Rye Bread

French Meadow 100% Rye with Flaxseed Bread

French Meadow European Sourdough Rye

French Meadow 100% Rye Bread with Sunflower Sead

French Meadow Whole Grain Rice Bread

Hazelsauer Sunflower Kernel Bread

Hazelsauer Two Grain Bread

Hazelsauer Whole Rye Bread

Germine Bavarian Organic Flaxseed Bread

Germine Bavarian Organic Multi-Grain Bread

Germine Bavarian Organic Pumpernickel Bread

Germine Bavarian Organic Whole Rye Bread

La Louisiane Sugar Free Baked Goods, Kenner, Louisiana

Lifestream Essence Bread- Sprouted/Unleavened Whole Wheat

Lotus Bakery German Rye

Mestemacher Pumpernickel

Pepperidge Farms Pumpernickel Bread

Pepperidge Farms Rye Bread

Pepperidge Farms Party Dark Pumpernickel Bread

Pepperidge Farms Party Jewish Rye Bread

Rudolph's 100% Rye Bread with Whole Grain

Ryvita Tasty Dark Rye Whole Grain Crisp Bread

Ryvita Toasted Sesame Rye Whole Grain Crisp Bread

Cakes, Brown Rice

Konriko Brown Rice Cakes

Lundberg Family Farms Brown Rice Cakes

Candy

Eda's Naturally Sweeetened Sugar Free Hard Candies

Estee Sugar Free Hard Candies

Fifty 50 Sugar Free Hard Candy

Sweet 'N Low Sugar Free Hard Candies

Capers

Cento Capers

Crosse & Blackwell Capers

Fancifood Capers

Goya Capers

Haddon House Capers

Haddon House Imported Non-Pareil Capers

Mezzeta Capers

Reese Capers

Roland Capers

Safeway Capers

San Marc Capers

Star Capers

Victoria Capers

Zatarain's Capers

Cereals, Whole Grains

Arrowhead Mills Bits 'O Barley

Arrowhead Mills Pearled Barley

Goya Pearled Barley

Quaker Pearled Barley

Arrowhead Mills Old Fashioned Prairie Oats

Arrowhead Mills Steel Cut Oats
Arrowhead Mills Oat Bran
Mother's 100% Natural Hot Cereal
  Whole Wheat/Rolled Wheat
Hodgson Mills Oat Bran Hot Cereal
Kellogg's Extra Fiber All Bran
Quaker Oat Bran Hot Cereal
Arrowhead Mills Old Fashioned Oat
  Meal
John McCann's Irish Oatmeal (not
  instant)
Old Wessex Ltd. Irish Style Oatmeat
Quaker Oatmeal (not instant)
Safeway Old Fashioned Oatmeal
Scottish Oatmeal
Food Club Old Fashioned Oats
Kountry Fresh Old Fashioned Oats
Quaker Oats
Kashi, The Breakfast Pilaf
Puffed Kashi
Puffed Kashi Seven Whole Grain and
  Sesame
Uncle Sam Cereal
Bob's Red Mill Stone Ground Cracked
  Wheat Hot Cereal
Hodgson Mills Cracked Wheat Hot
  Cereal
Bob's Red Mill Seven Grain Hot Cereal
Bob's Red Mill Stone Ground Whole
  Wheat Farina Hot Cereal
America's Choice Shredded Wheat
Arrowhead Mills Bite Size Shredded
  Wheat
Barbara's Shredded Wheat
Nabisco Shredded Wheat
Post Shredded Wheat

Chips and Sticks

Klondike Goldfingers Sweet Poato
  Sticks with Peanuts

Klondike Goldfingers Sweet Poato
  Sticks with Almonds
Klondike Goldfingers Sweet Poato
  Sticks with Cashew Halves
Lentil Chips: Original Recipe, Garlic
  Masala, Spice 'N Pepper
Terra Sweet Potato Chips
Zapp's Sweet Potato Chips

Chocolate

Baker's Unsweetened Chocolate Squares
Cuana Chocolate
Ghirardelli Premium Unsweetened Cocoa
Hershey's Unsweetened Baking
  Chocolate
Hershey's 100% Cocoa
Hershey's European Style Dutch
  Processed Cocoa
LeNoir American Chocolate
Lindt 70% Cocoa Chocolate Bar
Nestle Unsweetened Baking Chocolate
Orinico Chocolate
Valvrona Chocolate

Chocolate Mix

Carnation No Sugar Added Hot Cocoa
  Mix
Food Club Hot Cocoa Mix, No Sugar
  Added
Swiss Miss Diet Hot Chocolate

Cooking Oils

Canola Oils

America's Choice Canola Oil
Astor Canola Oil
Crisco Puritan Canola Oil
Food Club Canola Oil
Lorina Canolive Oil
Lou Ana Canola Oil
Mazola Canola Oil

Mrs. Tucker's Canola Oil
Shur Fine Canola Oil
Spectrum Naturals Canola Oil
Wesson Canola Oil
Whole Food Canola Oil
Corn Oil
America's Choice Corn Oil
Crisco Corn Oil
Delchamp's Corn Oil
Food Club Corn Oil
Mazola Corn Oil
Mrs. Tucker's Corn Oil
Shur Fine Corn Oil
Wesson Corn Oil
Peanut Oil
Astor Peanut Oil
Duke's Peanut Oil
Food Club Peanut Oil
Lorina Peanut Oil
Lou Ana Peanut Oil
Shur Fine Peanut Oil
Safflower Oil
Hain Safflower Oil
Hollywood Safflower Oil
Lou Ana Safflower Oil
Wesson Safflower Oil
Vegetable Oil
America's Choice Vegetable Oil
Blue Plate Vegetable Oil
Chef Way Vegetable Oil
Crisco Vegetable Oil
Food Club Vegetable Oil
Lou Ana Vegetable Oil
Mrs. Tucker's Vegetable Oil
Shur Fine Vegetable Oil
Wesson Vegetable Oil
Miscellaneous Oil
Crisco Flavored Oils
Dynasty Oriental Seasonal Oil
Dynasty Seasame Seed Oil
Dynasty Stir Fry Oil
Hain Walnut Oil
Lorina Basil Flavored Oil

Lorina Garlic Flavored Oil
Stonewall Kitchen Roasted Garlic Oil
Stonewall Kitchen Hot Chili Oil

Cooking Sprays
Baker's Joy Cooking Spray
Crisco Cooking Spray
Mazola Cooking Spray
Naturally Canola Cooking Spray
Naturally Garlic Cooking Spray
Naturally Olive Oil Cooking Spray
Pam Cooking Spray
Shur Fine Cooking Spray
Savor's Choice Cooking Spray
Spectrum Naturals Skillet Spray Canola
    Oil
Spectrum Naturals Skillet Spray Super
    Canola
Spectrum Naturals Skillet Spray Olive
    Oil
Sunola Canola Cooking Spray
Tryson House Butter Cooking Spray
Tryson House Garlic Cooking Spray
Tryson House Olive Cooking Spray
Weight Watcher's Canola Cooking Spray
Wesson Cooking Spray

Cooking Wines
Reese Maitre Jacques Burgundy
    Cooking Wine
Reese Maitre Jacques Vintage Cooking
    Wine
Regina Sherry Cooking Wine

Crackers and Rice Cakes
Bran a Crisp
Crostini-Tuscan Cracker With Stone
    Ground Whole Wheat
Konriko Brown Rice Cakes
Lundberg Family Farms Brown Rice
    Cakes
Wasa Fiber Rye

Wasa Light Rye
Wasa Multigrain
Wasa Sourdough Rye
Hol Grain Brown Rice Crackers
San-J Black Sesame Rice Cracker
San-J Sesame Brown Rice Crackers
San-J Tamari Brown Rice Crackers
Edward and Sons Brown Rice Snaps,
   Onion Garlic
Edward and Sons Brown Rice Snaps,
   Tamari Seasame
Edward and Sons Brown Rice Snaps,
   Unsalted Sesame
Edward and Sons Brown Rice Snaps,
   Vegetable
Finn Crisp Dark
Finn Crisp Dark with Caraway
Kavli All Natural Whole Grain
   Crispbread Crispy Thin and Hearty
   Thick
Kavli All Natural Whole Grain Garlic
Nabisco Triscuit Original
Nabisco Triscuit Low Sodium
Ryvita Whole Grain Crisp Bread, Tasty
   Light Rye
Ryvita Whole Grain Crisp Bread, Tasty
   Dark Rye
Safeway Woven Wheat Crackers
Whole Foods Baked Woven Wheats
Westbrae Natural Unsalted Brown Rice
   Wafers
Westbrae Natural Sesame Brown Rice
   Wafers

Dips

Bearitos Black Bean Dip
Cedarland Roasted Eggplant & Red
   Pepper Dip
Desert Pepper Black Bean Dip-Spicy
Granny Goose Jalapeno Bean Dip

Guiltless Gourmet Bean Dip, Mild and
   Spicy
Haig's Baba Ghannouge Eggplant Dip
Native Kjalii Fire Roasted Guacamole
Pezzini Farms Lemon Dill Dipping
   Sauce
Senor Felix's Guacamole
Whole Foods Pinto Bean Dip
Wildwood Baba Ghannouge Dip

Evaporated Milk

Carnation Evaporated Milk
Pet Evaporated Milk

Extracts

McCormick Extracts: Almond, Banana,
   Butter, Coconut, Lemon, Mint,
   Orange, Strawberry, Vanilla, Black
   Walnut
Shur Fine Lemon Extract
Trader's Choice Pure Lemon Extract
Zatarain's Root Beer Extract
Melipone Mexican Vanilla
Shur Fine Vanilla
Valu Time Vanilla
Zatarain's Vanilla

Flours

Arrowhead Mills Brown Rice Flour
Hodgson Mill Brown Rice Flour
Arrowhead Mills Barley Flour
Arrowhead Mills Buckwheat Flour
Bob's Red Mill Fava Bean Flour
Bob's Red Mill Stone Ground Garbanzo
   Bean Flour
Arrowhead Mills Oat Flour
Hodgson Mill Oat Bran Blend Flour
Arrowhead Mills Stone Ground Whole
   Wheat Flour

Bob's Red Mill Stone Ground Whole Wheat Flour

Bob's Red Mill Stone Ground Whole Wheat Pastry Flour

Hodgson Mill Whole Grain Stone Ground Whole Wheat Pastry Flour

Hodgson Mill Whole Grain Stone Ground Whole Wheat Flour

Arrowhead Mills Rye Flour

Bob's Red Mill Stone Ground Dark Rye Flour

Arrowhead Mills Whole Grain Rye Flour

Hodgson Mill Whole Grain Rye Flour

Arrowhead Mills Soy

Arrowhead Mills Spelt

Fruit, Canned

All Brands Canned Fruit Packed in Water or Natural Juices

Lucky Leaf Sliced Apples

America's Choice Unsweetened Old Fashioned Applesauce

Leroux Creek Apple-Apricot Sauce

Leroux Creek Apple-Berry Sauce

Leroux Creek Apple-Cherry Sauce

Leroux Creek Apple-Cinnamon Sauce

Lucky Leaf Old Fashion Natural Applesauce

Santa Cruz Organic Apple Sauce

Santa Cruz Organic Apple Blackberry Sauce

Santa Cruz Organic Apple Apricot Sauce

Santa Cruz Organic Apple Cinnamon Sauce

Solana Gold Organic Gravenstein Applesauce

Solana Gold Organic Gravenstein Boysenberry Applesauce

Solana Gold Organic Gravenstein Blackberry Applesauce

S&W Gravenstein Applesauce

Vermont Village Apricot Applesauce

Vermont Village Cranberry Applesauce

Whole Food Organic Unsweetened Applesauce

Columbia George Apricot Halves

Columbia George Pitted Cherries

S&W Natural Style Grapefruit Sections

S&W Natural Style Mandarin Orange Sections

America's Choice Lite Peaches

Del Monte Fruit Naturals Sliced Peaches

Food Club Peaches

Shur Fine Peaches, in Natural Juices

Thrifty Maid Peaches

America's Choice Lite Pears

Astor Lite Pears

Columbia George Organic Pear Halves

Del Monte Pear Halves

Food Club Pears

Shur Fine Pears, in Natural Juices

Thrifty Maid Pears

Fruit, Frozen

Food Club Whole Blackberries

Safeway Blackberries

Stilwell Blackberries

Food Club Whole Blueberries

Safeway Blueberries

Stilwell Blueberries

Food Club Honey Dew and Cantaloupe Melon Balls

Food Club Sliced Peaches

McKenzie's Peaches

Southern Sliced Peaches

Safeway Raspberries

Food Club Whole Strawberries

Safeway Strawberries

Southern Whole Strawberries
Stilwell Strawberries
Cascadian Farms Frozen Fruit
Whole Foods 365 Frozen Fruit

Fruit, Juice
Flavorite Lemon Juice
Real Lemon Lemon Juice
Real Lime Lime Juice

Fruit, Spreads
American Spoon Spreadable Fruit, "Spoon Fruit"
Bionaturae 100% Fruit
Clearbrook Farms Spreadable Fruit
Community Kitchens Fruit Spread
Dickerson's Purely Fruit
Estee Fruit Spread
Fifty 50 Fruit Spread
Fiordi Frutta 100% Fruit
La Don's Fancy Fruit Spread
Polaner All Fruit
R. W. Knudsen All Natural Fancy Fruit Spread
Smucker's Simple Fruit
Sorrell Ridge 100% Fruit
St. Dalfour 100% Fruit
The New Organic Co. - Conserve - Golden Apple, Mediterranean, Red Orange, Raspberry, Strawberry
Whole Foods 365 100% Fruit

Gelatin
Jell-O Sugar Free Low Calorie Gelatin Snacks
Knox's Unflavored Gelatin

Horseradish
Captain Toady's Hardy Horseradish Sauce
Kraft Horseradish, Prepared
Silver Spring Horseradish, Prepared
Sophia Clikas Horseradish, Prepared
Zatarain's Horseradish, Prepared

Hot Sauces
All Cajun Food Co. Andre's Rouge Spiced Pepper Sauce
Amazon Pepper Fiery Green Sauce
Café Tequila San Francisco Cayenne Red Hot Sauce
Cajun Chef Hot Sauce
Cajun Chef Green Hot Sauce
Cajun Rush Infinite Heat Xoo
Cajun Rush Pepper Sauce
Cajun Sunshine Hot Sauce
Chef Hans Hot Sauce
Chef Prudhomme's Pepper Sauce
CheRith Valley Gardens Hot Pepper Sauce
Colavita Classic Hot Sauce
Crystal Classic Cayenne Garlic Sauce
Crystal Classic Cayenne Pepper Sauce
Crystal Hot Sauce
El Fenix Hot Sauce
Frontera Tangy Toasted Arbol Hot Sauce
Gardens-by-the-Bay Hot Chile Oil
Hooters Hot Sauce
Louisiana Hot Sauce
"Louisiana" The Perfect Hot Sauce
Louisiana Gold Hot Sauce
Louisiana Gold Pepper Hot Sauce
The Original Louisiana Hot Sauce
Marie Sharp's Hot Sauce
Melinda's Hot Sauce
Shur Fine Hot Sauce
Sylvia's Hot Sauce

The Pepper Plant-Hot Pepper Sauce
Picu Pica Real Mexican Style Hot Sauce
Tabasco Hot Sauce
Trappey's Louisiana Hot Sauce
V.G. Buck Hot Balsamic Sauce
Whole Foods Organic Hot Sauce
Yucatan Sunshine Habenero Pepper
    Sauce

Hot Wing Sauces
Beano's Chicken Wing Sauce
Bob Baumhower's Wings—Extra Hot
    Wing Sauce
Jim Beam Wing Sauce

Hummus
Affi's Caper Hummus
Cedarland Roasted Garlic Hummus
Cedarland Roasted Red Pepepr
    Hummus
Cedarland Basil & Sundried Tomato
    Hummus
Cedarland Cilantro & Jalapeno
    Hummus
Choice of Vermont Hummus
Fantastic Foods Hummus
Frieda's Hummus, Traditional Flavor
    and Zesty Garlic
Haig's Hummus
Haig's Spicy Hummus
Haig's Hummus with Fire Roasted
    Pepper
Maranatha Hummus
Melissa's Black Bean Hummous
Melissa's Red Pepper Hummous
Meza Hummus with Roasted Eggplant
Meza Hummus with Roasted Garlic
Out to Lunch Hummus
Raquel's Middle Eastern Baba
    Ghannouge Hummus
Raquel's Middle Eastern Roasted Red
    Pepper Hummus

Raquel's Middle Eastern Spicy Hummus
Raquel's Middle Eastern Sun Dried
    Tomato Hummus
Swan Gardens Hummus
Tribe of Two Shieks Hummus: With
    Forty Spices, Garden Vegetable,
    Jalapeno With Roasted Garlic, Fresh
    Onion, Roasted Red Peppers
Wildwood Natural Foods — Low Fat
    Hummus
Wildwood Natural Foods Mid Eastern
    Hummus
Wildwood Natural Foods Spicy Low
    Fat Hummus

Ice Cream
Brown's Velvet Ice Cream - No Sugar
    Added
SugarLo Dietetic Ice Cream

Ketchup and Seafood Sauces
Captain Toady's Classic Cocktail Sauce
Captain Toady's Tasty Tartar Sauce
Estee Sugar Free Ketchup
Robbie's Ketchup
Stacy's Remoulade Sauce
Westbrae Unsweetened Un-Ketchup

Marinades and Sauces
Annie's Natural Mushroom Sauce
Annie's Vermont Cheddar Cheese Sauce
Cherchies Champagne Sauce for All
    Seasons, Marinade or Seafood Pasta
Drew's Kalamata Olive & Caper
    Marinade
Drew's Smoked Tomato Marinade
The Garlic Survival Co.-Roasted Garlic
    Marinade
Joe Beef's Greek Lemon Marinade
Grand Mere Garlic Recipe Marinade

Napa Valley BBQ Co. Sage Marinade
Nellie and Joe's Mojo Crillo Marinade
Pape Demos Lemon Herb Marinade
Postilion Bordeaux Wine Marinade
TAJ Bombay Curry Simmer Sauce
TAJ Calcutta Masala Simmer Sauce
TAJ Kashmiri Tandoori Marinade Sauce

Mayonnaise, Aioli & Tartar Sauce

Captain Tordy's Tasty Tartar Sauce
Consorzio Basil Flavored Olive Oil
  Mayonnaise
Consorzio Roasted Garlic Flavored
  Olive Oil Mayonnaise
Duke's Homemade Style Mayonnaise-
  Sugar Free
Jeremiah's Roasted Garlic Aioli
Life in Provence Aioli Provencal Garlic
  Mayonnaise
Miso Mayonnaise
Whole Foods Canola Oil Mayonnaise

Meat, Canned

Hormel Canned Chicken
Hormel Breast of Chicken
Swanson's Canned Chicken
Swanson's White Chicken
Swanson's Chunk Chicken
Swanson's White Chicken in Water
Swanson's Premium Chunk Chicken
  Breast
Swanson's Premium White and Dark
  Chicken
Sweet Sue Canned White Chicken
Valley Fresh White Chicken
Valley Fresh Chunk Chicken
Underwood Liverwurst Spread
Hormel Canned Turkey
Hormel White Turkey
Swanson's Canned Turkey

Meat, Sausage and Salami

Aidells Smoked Turkey & Chicken
  Sausage with Sun Dried Tomatoes
Black Forest Brand Ham
Columbus Cooked Corned Beef
Creole Country Green Onion Smoked
  Sausage with Crayfish
Creole Country Smoked Alligator Sauce
Creole Country Smoked Chaurice Sausage
D'Antonio's Hot Beef Patties
D'Antonio's Hot Links
D'Antonio's Italian Sausage with Beef
Gwaltney Bacon
Han's All Natural Sonoma Brand
  Chicken Sausage
Han's All Natural Sonoma Brand
  Chicken Sausage With Fresh Basil
  and Sun-Dried Tomatoes
Han's All Natural Sonoma Brand
  Chicken Sausage With Fresh Spinach
  & Feta Cheese
Hormel Genoa Salami
Manda Supreme Deli Style Sausage
Marciente's Duck and Pork Sausage
Marciente's Green Onion Sausage
Marciente's Italian Sausage with Beef
Marciente's Pheasant Pork Sausage
Marciente's Rabbit and Pork Sausage
Martin's Country Smoked Andouille
  Sausage
Martin's Pork Tasso
Martin's Smoked Sausage, Mild and Hot
Shelton's Cooked Uncured Chicken
  Franks
Shelton's Italian Sausage
Shelton's Cooked Uncured Turkey Burgers
Shelton's Cooked Uncured Turkey
  Franks: Smoked or Mild Flavor
Shelton's Turkey Sausage Patties
Note: Most Store-Made Sausage Is
  Acceptable

Mustards

Dry

Colman's Dry Mustard
Maille Dry Mustard with Horseradish

Brown, Creole & Hot

Arnaud's Sauce - Original Creole
 Remoulade
Ba-Tampte Delicatessen Style Mustard
Creole Delicacies Creole Mustard
Cottage Delight English Mustard with
 Horseradish
Finless Organic Whole Grain Mustard
French's Bold & Spicy Mustard
French's Hearty Deli Mustard
Grey Poupon Peppercorn Mustard
Horseshoe Creole Mustard
Luzianne Creole Mustard
McIlhenny Farms Mustard Coarse
 Ground
Crystal Brown Mustard, Pure Prepared
Crystal Spicy Brown Mustard
Grey Poupon Deli Mustard
Grey Poupon Spicy Brown Mustard
Guilden's Spicy Brown Mustard
Jack Daniel's Spicy Brown Mustard
Koop's Spicy Brown Mustard
Kosciusko Spicy Brown Mustard
McIlhenny Farms Spicy Brown Mustard
Napa Valley Mustard Co. Whole
 Ground Mustard
Nathan's Deli Style Mustard
Natural Value Stone Ground Mustard
Noyo Reserve Jalapeno Mustard
Plochman's Natural Stone Ground
 Mustard
Rex Creole Mustard
Sierra Nevada Stout and Stone Ground
 Mustard
Sierra Nevada Porter and Spicy Brown
 Mustard
Temeraire Green Peppercorn Mustard
Temeraire Old-Fashioned Mustard

Tulkoff Polish Mustard
Westbrae Natural Stone Ground
 Mustard
Whole Foods Organic German Mustard
Zatarain's Creole Mustard

Yellow

Crystal Yellow Mustard
French's Classic Yellow Mustard
All Cajun Food Co. T-Loui's Chow
 Chow
Horseshoe Chow Chow Mustard
Horseshoe French Style Mustard
Hunt's Gourmet Mustard
Natural Value Prepared Yellow
 Mustard
Safeway Select 100% Natural Yellow
Whole Foods Organic Yellow Mustard
Zatarain's Chow Chow

Dijon and Horseradish Mustard

Amora Dijon
Book Binder's Hot Horseradish
 Mustard
Danish Blue Dijon Blend
Don's Mountain Herb Dijon Mustard
Edmond Fallot Green Peppercorn Dijon
Edmond Fallot Tarragon Dijon
Edmond Fallot Basil Dijon
Edmond Fallot Seed Style Dijon
Finless Organic Dijon
Finless Organic Dijon Mustard with
 Lemon Flavour
French's Dijon Mustard
Grey Poupon Country Dijon
Grey Poupon Dijon Mustard
Jack Daniel's Dijon Mustard
Koop's Dijon Mustard
Koop's Horseradish Mustard
La Don's Gourmet Mustard
Maille Dijon Mustard with Horseradish
Moutarde de Lion Pommery Extra
 Strong Mustard
Safeway Select Dijon

Temeraire Dijon Mustard
Tulkoff Horseradish Mustard
Westbrae Natural Dijon Style Mustard
Whole Foods Organic Dijon Mustard
Flavored Mustards
Champ's Tarragon Mustard
Champ's Mustard with Fennel
Champ's Mustard with Herbs

Nuts and Seeds

Arrowhead Mills Almonds
Blue Diamond Almonds, Roasted and
  Plain
Blue Diamond Pistachios
Clement Faugier Whole Chestnuts
Energy Club Assorted Nuts
Fisher Nuts
Food Club Nuts
Hubs Peanuts
John Macadam Macadamia Nuts
Mauna Loa Macadamia Nuts
Maranatha Brand Almonds, Butternuts,
  Cashews, Macadamia, Pistachio
  Nuts & Sunflower Seeds
Planters Assorted Nuts, Roasted, Salted,
  Unsalted
Pumpkorn Pumpkin Seeds: Original,
  Chili, Curry
Roddenbery's Peanut Patch Green
  Boiled Peanuts
Shur Fine Assorted Nuts
Sun Flower Kernels
Sunshine Country Peanuts
Sunshine Country Pecans
Sunshine Country Pistachios
Sunshine Sunflower Seeds
Whole Foods Mission Almonds

Olives

All Brands Black, Green, Stuffed
America's Choice Olives

Armstrong Olives
Belladí Cerignola Olives
Bruno's Market Olives
Gil's Chardonnay Anchovy Olives
Gil's Chardonnay Stuffed Jalapeno
  Olives
Gil's Chardonnay Garlic Stuffed Olives
Oberti Olives
Olivies Napa Valley Mediterranean
  Green Olive Salad
Progresso Olive Salad
Peloponnese Kalamato Olives
Province de France Pitted Green Olives
Province de France Tiny Black
  "Nicoise" Olives
Province de France Old Cured Black
  Ripe Olives
Province de France French Green Olives
Domaine de Provence Olives
Haddon House Olives
Italbrand Calamata Olives
Italbrand Olives
Krino's Kalamata Olives
Lindsay Olives
Manzanilla Olives
Mario Olives
Mezzetta Pickled Olives
Mezzetta Greek Calamata Olives
Miss Scarlett's Olives
Peloponnese Atalanti Olives
Reese Olives
Roland Olives Stuffed with Anchovies
Roland Provencal Picholine Olives
Santa Barbara Olive Co.
Star Olives
Tabasco® Manzanilla Spanish Olives
Zatarain's Olives

Olive Oils

All Brands
Alessi Olive Oil

Bella Cucina Extra Virgin Olive Oil
Berio Olive Oil
Bertolli Olive Oil
Bionaturae Olive Oil
Boscoli Olive Oil
Carapelli Olive Oil
Casteluetrano Olive Oil
Colavita Olive Oil
Consorzio Basil Flavored Olive Oil
Consorzio Roasted Garlic Flavor
    Olive Oil
Consorzio Roasted Pepper Flavor
    Olive Oil
Consorzio Rosemary Flavored Olive Oil
Da Vinci Olive Oil
Filippo Berrio Olive Oil
Gardens-by-the-Bay Herbed Olive Oil
Goya Olive Oil
Greek Gourmet Olive Oil
Grey Poupon Olive Oil
James Plagriol Olive Oil
Kirlangic Lizma Zeytinyagi Olive Oil
Loriva Olive Oil
Master Choice Olive Oil
Melina's Olive Oil
Morea Olive Oil
Olio Santa Extra Virgin Olive Oil
Perfecto Herbed Olive Oil
Prestigio Olive Oil
Pompeian Olive Oil
Progresso Olive Oil
San Marc Olive Oil
Sasso Olive Oil
Spectrum Naturals Olive Oil
Ti'Amo Herbed Olive Oil
Vigo Olive Oil
Whole Foods Olive Oil
Whole Foods 365 Extra Virgin
    Olive Oil
Zuppardo Bros. Olive Oil

Pasta

Bionaturae Pasta
Castellana Rustic Italian Pasta
    "Trecce Nere"
Castellana Rustic Italian Pasta
    "Fusilli Tricolore"
De Cecco Spaghetti
Eden Organic Bell Pepper Basil Ribbons
Eden Organic Spinach Ribbons
Eden Organic Endless Tubes
Eden Organic Kamut Spirals
Eden Organic Golden Amber Durum
    Wheat Kamut Spirals Whole Grain
Eden Organic Golden Amber Durum
    Wheat Parsley Garlic Ribbons
Eden Organic Golden Amber Durum
    Wheat Pesto Ribbons
Fresina Pasta Co., Baton Rouge,
    Louisiana
Hodgson Mill Stone Ground Whole
    Wheat Pasta
Lundberg Organic Brown Rice Pasta
Mendocino Pasta Co. Italian Herb
    Linguine
Mendocino Pasta Co. Garlic Basil Angel
    Hair
Mendocino Pasta Co. Garlic Basil
    Fettuccine
Mendocino Pasta Co. Garlic Basil
    Penne
Mendocino Pasta Co. Tomato Basil
    Fettuccine
Pastariso Stone Ground Brown Rice
    Spirals
Pritikin Whole Durum Wheat Pasta
Thai Kitchen Red Curry Pasta
Westbrae Natural 100% Whole Durum
    Wheat Pasta
Whole Foods 365 100% Durum Wheat
    Semolina
Whole Foods Organic Durum Whole
    Wheat Pasta

Peanut Butter and Other Flavored Butters

Peanut Butter

Admas 100% Natural and No Stir Crunchy Peanut Butter
Arrowhead Mills Organic Peanut Butter
Fifty 50 No Sugar Added Peanut Butter
Laura Scudder's Old-Fashioned Peanut Butter
Maranatha Peanut Butter
Masters Choice All Natural Peanut Butter
Safeway Peanut Butter
Smuckers All Natural Peanut Butter
Tree of Life Organic Peanut Butter
Whole Foods Organic Peanut Butter
Whole Foods 365 Peanut Butter

Other Flavored Butters

Arrowheat Mills Organic Sesame Tahini Butter
I.M. Healthy Soy Nut Butter
Maranatha Almond Butter
Maranatha Cashew Butter
Maranatha Macadamia Butter
Maranatha Pistachio Butter
Maranatha Sesame Butter
Maranatha Sesame Tahini Butter
Maranatha Sunflower Butter
Whole Foods Organic Almond Butter
Whole Foods Organic Cashew Butter
Whole Foods Organic Sesame Tahini Butter

Peppers

Bruno's Wax Peppers, Hot, Nippy & Mild
Casa Fiesta Whole Green Chilies
Food Club Green Chilies
Old El Paso Green Chilies
Ortego Diced Green Chilies
Herdez Chilpotles

Pelloponnese Rainbow Peppers
Casa Fiesta Nacho Sliced Jalapenos
Goya Jalapeno Peppers
Hatch Select Sliced Jalapenos
Italbrand Roasted Peppers Italian Style
McIlhenny Farms Jalapeno Nacho Slices
Mezzetta Hot Cherry Peppers
Mezzetta Chili Peppers
Mezzetta Jalapeno Peppers
Mezzetta Pickled Peppers
Mezzetta Roasted Yellow & Red Sweet Peppers
Mission Jalapeno Peppers
Old El Paso Jalapeno Slices
Old El Paso Jalapeno Relish
Ortego Whole Jalapenos
Progresso Cherry Peppers
Progresso Tuscan Peppers
Mrs. Renfro's Jalapeno Peppers

Pickles

America's Choice Dill Pickles
America's Choice Dill Pickle Slices
Batampte Half Sour Pickles
Batampte Garlic Dill Pickles
Bubbies Kosher Dill Pickles
Cascadian Farms Kosher Dills
CheRith Valley Gardens Dill Pickles
CheRith Valley Gardens "Hot 'n Spicy" Dill Pickles
Clausen's Dill Pickles
Cosmic Cukes Dill Pickles
Food Club Dill Pickles
Ma Brown Pickles
Mt. Olive Dill Chips
Rainbo Dill Pickles
America's Choice Hamburger Slices
Deep South Hamburger Dill Pickles
Food Club Hamburger Dill Slices
Shur Fine Hamburger Dills

Valu Time Hamburger Dill Slices
Vlasic Hamburger Dill Chip Pickles
Amercia's Choice Kosher Pickles
Clausen's Kosher Dill Pickles
Deep South Kosher Dill Spears
Shur Fine Kosher Dills
Valu Time Kosher Dills
Vlasic Snack' MMs - Kosher Dill Pickles
Shur Fine No Garlic Dill Pickles
Deep South Whole Dill Pickles

Pimientos

Dromedary Sliced Pimientos
Goya Pimientos

Pine Nuts

Imported Alessi Pignoli Pine Nuts
Haddon House Imported Alessi Pignoli
    Pine Nuts
Haddon House Pine Nuts

Pretzels

Natural GH Foods Peanut Butter
    Pretzels, 100% Whole Wheat

Relish

Bubbies Pure Kosher Dill Relish
Cascadian Farms Dill Relish
Mt. Olive Dill Relish
Rainbo Dill Relish
Vlasic Dill Relish

Rice, Brown, Brown Basmati, & Wild

Not Instant - All Brands Long Grain
    Brown Rice
America's Choice Brown Rice
Arrowhead Brown Basmati Rice
Arrowhead Mills Brown Rice
Dynasty Extra Fancy Brown Rice

Hime Organic Brown Rice
Fantastic Food Brown Basmati Rice
Cache River Brown Basmati Rice
Konriko Brown Rice
Konriko Cajun Brown Rice Pilaf
Lundberg Family Farms California
    Long & Short Grain Brown Rice
Lundberg Wehani Brown Rice
Mahatma Brown Rice
Nutra-Farmed Lundberg Family Farms
    California Brown Basmati Rice
Nutra-Farmed Tilda Brown Basmati
    Rice
S&W Long Grain Brown Rice
Texmati Brown Basmati Rice
Uncle Ben's Brown Rice
Canadian Lake Wild Rice
California Harvest Wild Rice with
    Shitake Mushrooms
Grey Owl Wild Rice
Haddon House Extra Fancy Cultivated
    Wild Rice
Lake 100% Wild Rice
Mac Dougall's California Wild Rice

Salad Dressings

Annie's Naturals Caesar Dressing
Annie's Naturals Famous Garlic and
    Herb Salad Dressing
Annie's Naturals Goddess Dressing
Annie's Naturals Green Garlic Salad
    Dressing
Annie's Naturals Organic Horseradish
    Vinaigrette with Echamacea
Annie's Naturals Sea Veggie and Sesame
    Vinaigrette
Annie's Naturals Shitake and Sesame
    Vinaigrette
Annie's Naturals Smoked Tomato and
    Porcini Vinaigrette

Annie's Naturals Tuscany Italian Dressing

B. Felice and Sons Garlic Herb and Dill Dressing

Bernard Napa Valley Lemon Caesar Vinaigrette

Briana's Real French Vinaigrette

Brianna's Special Request: Rich Santa Fe Blend

Cabria-Country Balsamic Vinaigrette

California Harvest Chipotle & Lime Mustard with Roasted Garlic Dressing

California Harvest Green Olive & Lemon Mustard with Roasted Garlic Dressing

California Harvest Roasted Tomato and Balsamic with Roasted Garlic Dressing

Cardini's Herb Dressing & Marinade

Cardini's Italian Dressing & Marinade with Extra Virgin Olive Oil

Cardini's Lemon Herb Dressing & Marinade

Cardini's Lime Dill Dressing & Marinade

Cardini's Original Caesar Dressing

Cardini's Pesto Pasta Dressing

Cardini's Zesty Garlic Dressing & Marinade

Carmela's Vinaigrette Authentique

Carmela's Balsmaic Vinaigrette

Carmela's Provencale Vinaigrette

Chef Crozier Caesar Salad Dressing

Chef Crozier Vinaigrette

Drew's Roasted Garlic Dressing

Drew's Shitake Ginger Dressing

Drew's Smoked Tomato Dressing

Drew's Kalamata Olive & Caper Dressing

Gran'mere's Garlic Recipe Dressing

Drew's Lemon Tahini & Chive Dressing

Grey Poupon Italienne Vinaigrette

Isabella & Rae's Lemony Olive Dressing

Jardine's Green Olive Vinaigrette

la Madeleine la Vinaigrette Caesar Salad Dressing

La Martinque Bleu Cheese

La Martinque True French Vinaigrette

Live a Little-Real Caesar Dressing

Martin Bros. Classic Caesar

Martin Bros. Garlic Mustard Dressing

Napa Valley BBQ Co. Chardonnay Citrus Dressing

Napa Valley BBQ Co. Sage Dressing

Naturally Fresh Italian Herb Vinaigrette

Naturally Fresh Lite Ranch

Nellie and Joe's Mojo Criollo Marinade and Dressing

All Natural Newman's Own Olive Oil & Vinegar

Oak Farms Florentine Salad Dressing

Old Cape Cod Parmesan and Peppercorn

Old Cape Cod Garlic and Herb

The Perfect Caesar

Postilion Anchovies Vinaigrette

Postilion Moutarde Forte de Dijon Vinaigrette

Postilion Roquefort Fresh Creamy Vinaigrette

Provence Creamy Vinaigrette

Provence Sun Dried Tomato Vinaigrette

Safeway Select Blue Cheese Dressing

Sal and Judy's Bleu Cheese

Sal and Judy's Roasted Garlic

Sal and Judy's Italian Dressing

The Silver Palate Balsamic Country Salad Splash

The Silver Palate Julie's Caesar Salad Splash

The Silver Palate Pesto Grlic Salad Splash

The Silver Palate Pesto Garden Mustard
Dressing
Sonoma Gourmet Cubernet Vinaigrette
Sonoma Gourmet Chardonnay
Vinaigrette
Sonoma Gourmet Blue Cheese
Vinaigrette
Spectrum Naturals Blue Cheese Style
Spectrum Naturals Creamy Garlic
Spectrum Naturals Creamy Dill
Stonewall Kitchen Lemon Peppercorn
Vinaigrette
Stonewall Kitchen Roasted Red Pepper
Vinaigrette
The Source Herb French Dressing
Timpone's Fresh Sicilian Dressing &
Marinade
Whole Foods Caesar Dressing
Whole Foods Italian Vinaigrette
Whole Foods Lemon Tahini Dressing
Whole Foods Sesame Garlic Dressing

Salsa

Arribe Mexican Green Salsa
Cannon's Cannon Fire Salsa
Casa Sanchez Mild Salsa Roja
Casa Sanchez Hot Salsa Roja
Casa Sanchez Mild Salsa Verde
Chile Morita Fire Roasted Salsa
Del Monte Thick and Chunky Salsa
Desert Pepper 2 Olive Roasted Garlic
Salsa Medium Hot
Desert Pepper Divino Mild
Desert Pepper Corn Black Bean Roasted
Red Pepper Salsa
Desert Pepper Salsa del Rio: Medium &
Hot
El Paso Chile Co. Salsa
El Paso Chile Co. Mild Salsa Primera
El Paso Chile Co. Snake Bite Salsa Hot
Enrico's Chipotle Salsa

Enrico's Roasted Garlic Salsa
Flame Boy's Wild Ride Smoky Salsa
with Roasted Habanero Peppers
Flame Boy's Wild Ride Smoky Salsa
with Roasted Peppers and Onions
Food Club Thick and Chunky Salsa
Frontera Jalapeno Salsa
Frontera Habanero Salsa
Frontera Roasted Tomato Salsa
Garden of Eatin Hot Habanero Fiery
Salsa
Garden Valley Naturals Black Bean Salsa
Garden Valley Naturals Roasted Garlic
Salsa, Mild or Hot
Granny Goose Bear Salsa
Guiltless Gourmet Tomato Salsa
Guiltless Gourmet Roasted Pepper Salsa
Guiltless Gourmet Salsa
Herdez Salsa Casera
Herdez Salsa Ranchera
Herdez Salsa Verde
La Mexicana Salsa
Marie's Roasted Garlic Salsa
Mexi-Snax Salsa Douce, Salsa Mild
Mexi-Snax Salsa Epicée Salsa Hot
Muir Glen Chipotle Salsa
Muir Glen Garden Pepper Medley Salsa
Muir Glen Roasted Onion & Pepper
Salsa
Muir Glen Garlic Cilantro Salsa
Muir Glen Roasted Garlic Salsa
Native Kjalii Fire Roasted Red Salsa
Native Cucumber Salsa Fresca
Native Fire Roasted Green Salsa
Newman's Own Mild Salsa - Not
Medium
Old El Paso Garden Pepper Salsa
Old El Paso Thick-N-Chunky Salsa
Ortega Salsa
Pace Thick & Chunky Salsa with
Cilantro

Parrot Brand Salsas: Black Bean Organic, Chunky Organic, Roasted Garlic Organic, Sundried Tomato Organic, Tomatillo Organic
Rose Timpone's Recipe Salsa Muy Rica
Rose Timpone's Salsa
Salpica Mild Rustic Tomato Salsa
Salpica Hot Red Chipotle Salsa
Salpica Medium Garlicky Green Salsa
Santa Barbara Roasted Garlic Salsa
Simply Zinful Salsa
Sonora-Grande Salsa
The Garlic Survival Co. "Triple" Garlic Salsa
The Garlic Survival Co. Tomatillo Garlic Salsa
The Salsa Factory: Chi-Po-Te Madness, Garlic Sensational, Gourmet Blend Roasted Garlic
Whole Foods Salsas

Sauces, Barbecue
Basque Meat Tenderizer Barbecue Sauce
M. Eleana's Bar-Be-Que Sauce, Special Family Recipe, to order: (804) 282-7523

Sauces, Mexican
Frontera Roasted Poblano-Tomato
Las Palmas Enchilada Sauce
Las Palmas Red Chile Sauce

Sauces, Pasta
California Seasonings Cioppino & Pasta Sauce
Paladini Cioppino Sauce
Dell Amore Artichoke and Capers Pasta Sauce
San Remo Artichoke Heart Sauce
Classico di Napoli Tomato & Basil Pasta Sauce
Classico di Napoli Spicy Red Pepper Pasta Sauce

Del Amore Fresh Basil and Garlic Pasta Sauce
Enrico's Traditional Italian Style Pasta Sauce
Enrico's Traditional Italian Style Pasta Sauce with Peppers & Mushrooms
Garden Valley Organic Four Cheese Pasta Sauce
Muir Glen Organic Tomato Basil Pasta Sauce Fat Free
Paladini Tomato Basil Sauce
Pritikin Tomato Basil Pasta Sauce
Sinatra's Tomato Basil and Parmesan Cheese Pasta Sauce
Tommaso's Tomato Basil Pasta Sauce
Dell Amore Eggplant and Marinara Pasta Sauce
Jacques Pepin's Kitchen Champagne Sauce
Jacques Pepin's Kitchen Pasta Sauce
Jacques Pepin's Kitchen Tomato Provencale Sauce
Elena's Funghi Pepe Verde Pasta Sauce
Mediterranean Kalamata Marinara Sauce
Mediterranean Santorini Summer Sauce
Millina's Finest Fat Free Organic Garlic Pasta Sauce
Millina's Finest Organic Garlic & Basil Pasta Sauce
Millina's Finest Fat Free Organic Hot 'n Spicey Pasta Sauce
Millina's Finest Fat Free Organic Marinara Sauce
Millina's Marinara with Herbs Pasta Sauce
Millina's Pesto/Sundried Tomato Pasta Sauce
Millina's Finest FF Organic Sweet Pepper and Onion Pasta Sauce
Millina's Tomato Alfredo Pasta Sauce
Millina's Tomato and Basil Pasta Sauce

Millina's Tomato and Mushroom Pasta Sauce

Classico Roasted Peppers and Onion Pasta Sauce

Lagniappe Gourmet Roasted Sweet Red Pepper Sauce

Muir Glen Organic Cabernet Marinara Pasta Sauce Fat Free

Colavita Marinara

Colavita Marinara Classic Hot

Dell Amore Marinara Pasta Sauce

Dell Amore Spicey Marinara Sauce

Frutti Di Bosco Marinara Sauce

Patsy's Marinara Sauce

Pezzini Artichoke Marinara Sauce

Rao's Homemade Marinara Sauce

Sidari's Marinara Sauce

Sinatra's Milano Marinara Sauce

Sinatra's Mushroom Marinara Sauce

Thunder Bay Zucchini Marinara Sauce

Whole Foods Neopolitan Sauce: Marinara

Whole Foods 365 Marinara Sauce

Whole Foods 365 Roasted Garlic Sauce

Whole Foods 365 Pesto Sundried Tomato Sauce

Dell Amore Porcini Mushroom Pasta Sauce

Rising Moon Pasta Sauces

Whole Foods Organic Pasta Sauce Fat-Free

Whole Foods Organic Pasta Sauce

Muir Glen Organic Garlic and Onion Pasta Sauce Fat Free

Classico Roasted Garlic Pasta Sauce

Muir Glen Organic Roasted Garlic Pasta Sauce Fat Free

Thunder Bay Garlic and Pepper Pasta Sauce

Tommaso's Pasta Sauce Arrabbiata

Coyote Cocina New Mexico Red Chile Pasta Sauce

Coyote Cocina Yellow Chile Pasta Sauce

Rao's Homemade Arrabialta Sauce

Frutti Di Bosco Wild Chanterella Sauce

Frutti Di Bosco Truffle-Porcini Sauce

Rustichella d'abruzzo Arrabbiata Sauce

Frutti Di Bosco Puttanesca Sauce

Patsy's Puttanesca Sauce

Rao's Homemade Puttanesca Sauce

Rustichella d'abruzzo Puttanesca Sauce

Tommaso's Puttanesca Sauce

Rao's Homemade Siciliana Sauce

Whole Foods Apulian Sauce Diavoliccino, Hot

Whole Foods Roman Sauce Puttanesca

Whole Foods Roman Puttanesca with Olives, Capers and Anchovies

Hunt's Homestyle Spaghetti Sauce - No Sugar Added

Hunt's Homestyle Flavored Meat Spaghetti Sauce - No Sugar Added

Hunt's Homestyle Garlic and Herb Spaghetti Sauce - No Sugar Added

Hunt's Homestyle Spaghetti Sauce with Mushrooms - No Sugar Added

Mom's Spaghetti Sauce

Timpone's Classic Spaghetti Sauce

Newman's Own Tomato Diavolo Spicy Sauce for Pasta, Chicken, etc.

Muir Glen Organic Sun-Dried Tomatoes Pasta Sauce Fat Free

Elena's Bread Dipping Sauce - Spicey Tomato and Herb

Sauces, Pesto

Bella Cucina Olivada Olive Pesto

Bella Cucina Sun-Dried Tomato Pesto

Cardine's Pesto Sauce with Basil and Extra Virgin Olive Oil

Fox's Fine Foods Arugula, Roasted
  Garlic and Artichoke Pesto
Fox's Fine Foods Fine Roasted
  Vegetable Pesto
Fox's Fine Foods Roasted Onion Pesto
  with Lemon and Rosemary
Fox's Fine Foods Yellow Sun-Dried
  Tomato Pesto with Fennel and Basil
Master Choice Red Pepper Pesto Sauce
Master Choice Sun-Dried Tomato
  Pesto Sauce
Melissa's Sun-Dried Tomato Pesto
Pezzini Farms Artichoke Pesto
Sanremo Pesto
Sidari's Pesto Sauce
Sonoma Pesto
The Garlic Survival Co. - Garlic Pesto
The Grower's Co. Nouvelle Garni
  Selection Pesto Basil Sauce and
  Seasoning Concentrate
Tex France Pesto
Tex France Sun-Dried Tomato Pesto

Sauces, Picante

Food Club Mexican Style Picante Sauce
Old El Paso Picante Sauce
Pace Picante Salsa
Pace Picante Sauce
The New Organics Co. Authentic
  Mexican Picante
Tapatio-Salsa Picante Hot Sauce

Sauces, Pizza

Gold Whisk Pizza Sauce
Muir Glen Organic Pizza Sauce
Whole Foods Apulian Sauce
  Diavoliccino, Hot

Sauces, Soy

Kikkoman Soy Sauce
Shoyu Soy Sauce

Tabasco Soy Sauce
Tamari Soy Sauce
Tamari Soy Sauce Natural
Tamari Soy Sauce Wheat Free
Yamasa Soy Sauce

Seafood, Canned

Clams and Clam Juice

Cento Minced Clams
Chicken of the Sea Baby Clams
Chicken of the Sea Clams
Crown Prince Baby Clams
Doxee Minced Clams
Geisha Baby Clams
Great Award Smoked Clams
Orleans Clams
Orleans All Natural Clam Juice
Progresso Minced Clams
Reese Smoked Baby Clams
Reese All Natural Clam Juice
Roland Baby Clams
Snow's Clams

Crabmeat

Chicken of the Sea Crabmeat
Crown Prince Crabmeat
Orleans Canned Crabmeat
Reese Crabmeat

Fish

Chicken of the Sea Jack Mackeral
Reese Naturally Smoked Fillets of
  Kippered Herring

Mussels

Reese Mussels in Red Sauce
Ty Ling Smoked Mussels

Oysters

Chicken of the Sea Canned Smoked
  Oysters
Chicken of the Sea Oysters
Crown Prince Smoked Oysters
Empress Whole Oysters
Geesha Whole Oysters

Great Award Smoked Oysters
Orleans Canned Whole Oysters
Orleans Smoked Oysters
Reese Smoked Oysters
Reese Whole Boiled Oysters
Salmon
America's Choice Salmon
Chicken of the Sea Salmon
Chicken of the Sea Pink Salmon
Chicken of the Sea Red Salmon
Double Q Pink Salmon
Food Club Salmon
Master Choice Salmon
Miramonte Pink Salmon
Pillar Rock Salmon
Pink Beauty Salmon
Reese Whole Pink Salmon
Roland Salmon
Sardines
Bono Sardines
Brunswick Holmes Sardines, Spring
   Water or Soybean Oil & Seasoned
   with Peppers
Crown Prince Sardines
Haddon House Sardines
Holmes Sardines
King Oscar Sardines
Port Clyde Sardines
Reese Sardines in Garlic Sauce
Roland Sardines
Tiny Tots Sardines
Underwood Sardines
Vigo Sardines
Shrimp
Chicken of the Sea Shrimp
Orleans Canned Shrimp
Reese Tiny Shrimp
Snails
Reese Pre-Cooked Snails
Tuna
America's Choice Tuna

Breast o' Chicken Tuna
Bumble Bee Tuna
Chicken of the Sea Tuna
Dave's Solid White Albacore Tuna,
   Garlic and Gourmet Style
Deep Sea Tuna
Food Club Tuna
Hormel Tuna
Master Choice Tuna
Miramonte Tuna
Natural Sea Tuna
Shur Fine Tuna
Star Kist Tuna
Swanson's Tuna
Tree of Life Tongol Tuna
Whole Foods Chunk Light Tongol Tuna
Whole Foods Solid White Albacore
   Tuna
Whole Foods 365 Solid White Albacore
   Tuna

Seasonings, Spices, Herbs
All Purpose and Herbed Seasonings
Accent Flavor Enhancer
Aux Anysetiers Du Roy Ground Pepper
   with Herbs of Provence
Durkee's Herb Seasoning
Great Shakes Peppercorn Medley
McCormick California Style Blend
   Onion Powder and Minced Onion
McCormick Fine Herbs
McCormick Flavor Enhancer
McCormick Salt 'n Spice
Miss Ruth's All Natural Seasoning
Only in New Orleans Herb Spice
Morton's Nature Seasons
Mrs. Dash Extra Spicy Onion & Herb
Schilling Salad Supreme Seasoning
Spike All Purpose Natural Seasoning
Tony Chachere Special Herb Blend

Barbecue & Southwest Seasonings
The Essence of Emeril Southwest Spice
McCormick Barbecue Seasoning
Rex Barbecue Seasoning
The Spice Hunters Hickory Barbecue
The Spice Hunters Mesquite
Talko's Texas Liquid Smoke
Wright's Natural Hickory Seasoning
    Liquid Smoke

Cajun Seasonings, Creole and Spicy
All Cajun Food Co. Bruce's Blend
    Sydeco Seasoning
Arise's Seasoning
Andy Roo's Cajun Jambalaya Creole
    Seasoning
Applewood Herb Farm Premium Blend
    Seasonings
Chef Paul Prudhomme's Magic
    Seasoning Blends
Delaune's Cajun – All Seasoning
Grandma Rena's All Purpose Cajun
    Spices
Johnny's Seasoning Salt
La Spice All Purpose Seasoning
Bayou Bang Cajun Seasoning
Cajun's Choice Creole Seasoning
Cajun Classique Cajun Seasoning
Cajun Land Cajun Seasoning with
    Green Onions
Louisiana Cajun Seasoning
Tony Chachere's Cajun More Spice
    Seasonings
Chef Hans Louisiana Creole Seasoning
Konriko Creole Seasoning
The Essence of Emeril Bayou Blast
The Spice Hunters Jamaican Jerk Blend
Szeged Hungarina Hot (& Plain)
    Paprika
Tony Chachere's Creole Seasoning
Tony Chachere's Extra-Lite

Garlic Seasonings
McCormick California Style Blend
    Garlic Powder and Minced Garlic
Mediterranean Inspirations Marinated
    Garlic
Spice World Garlic and Pepper
    Seasoning Salt
The Garlic Survival Co.: Garlic
    Pepper 'n Spices, Garlic Salt &
    Parsley, Garlic Powder & Spices

Italian Seasonings
Drogheeria & Alimentari Seasonings of
    Italy
Durkee's Italian Seasoning
Great Shakes Italian Seasoning
McCormick Italian Seasoning
Rex Italian Seasoning
San Marc Italian Style Granulated
    Garlic
Sonoma Sun Dried Italian Seasoning
Spice Hunter Italian Seasoning
Spice World Italian Seasoning
Tone's Italian Seasoning
Trader's Choice Italian Seasoning

Lemon Seasonings
Spice Island Lemon Herb Seasoning
Spice World Lemon and Pepper
    Seasoning Salt
The Spice Hunters Lemon Grass
Tone's Lemon-Pepper

Meat Seasonings
Cajun Land Meat Seasoning
Durkee's Steak Sauce
The Essence of Emeril Rustic Rub
McCormick Grill Mates Montreal Steak
Only in New Orleans Brisket Rub
Great Shakes Grilled Steak Seasoning

Mexican Seasonings
Bush's Chili Magic Traditional Style
Garlic Capital Products South of the
    Border Mix

Mexene Chili Powder
Pico de Gallo Mexican Seasoning
Tabasco® 7-Spice Chili Recipe
The Spice Hunters Fajita Seasoning

Oriental & Curry Seasonings

Instant India Authentic Curry Paste
La Don's Chinese Red Pepper
Madra's Curry Powder
McCormick Chinese 5 Spice
The Spice Hunters Chinese Five Spices
The Spice Hunters Stir Fry Ginger
The Spice Hunters Hot Curry Seasoning
Thai Kitchen Green Curry Paste
Thai Kitchen Red Curry Paste

Pizza Seasonings

Chef Paul Pruddomme's Pizza & Pasta
   Herb Magic
Great Shakes Pizza Seasoning
McCormick Classic Pizza Seasoning
McCormick Spicy Pizza Seasoning
Spice Hunter Pizza Seasoning

Poultry Seasonings

Cajun Land Poultry Seasoning
Napa Valley BBQ Co. Poultry Grilling
   Spice & Rub
McCormick Grill Mates Chicken
McCormick Herb Chicken Seasoning
McCormick Gourmet Spice Poultry
   Seasoning
McCormick Poultry Seasoning
McCormick Rotisserie Chicken
   Seasoning
Rex Poultry Seasoning
Schilling Poultry Seasoning
Spice Island Poultry Seasoning
The Spice Hunters Poultry
The Spice Hunters Poultry Grill and
   Broil

Seafood Seasonings

Cajun Classiques Blackened Seasoning
Cajun's Choice Blackened Seasoning

California-Mediterranean Pisto's
   Sensational Blackening Seasoning
Cajun King Lemon Butter Amandine
   Seasoning
Frank Davis strictly N'Awlins
   Seasoning: "Bronzing," "Sprinkling
   Spice" Seafood
Napa Valley BBQ Co. Seafood Grilling
   Spice & Rub
Le Cordon Bleu Seasoning For Grilled
   Fish
The Spice Hunters Fish Seasoning
Rex Blackened Seasoning
Zatarain's Blackened Fish Seasoning
Andy Roo's Louisiana BBQ Shrimp
   Creole Seasoning
Cajun King Barbecued Shrimp
   Seasoning
McCormick Cajun Quick Spicy Shrimp
   Seasoning
Shrimp Mosca Seasoning Blend
Cajun Land Crab Boil
Louisiana "Fish Fry Products" Crab
   Boil
New Orleans Crawfish, Shrimp and
   Crab Boil
Rex Crab Boil
Zatarain's Crab Boil
Zatarain's Gumbo Filé

Vegetable Seasonings

The Essence of Emeril Vegetable Dust
The Spice Hunters Vegetable Seasoning

Salt Free

Bayou Bang Gourmet Cajun Spices –
   Salt Free, All Natural Ingredients
Captain Mike's Seasoning No Salt and
   Extra Spicey
Estee Sodium Free Salt It
McCormick Saltless
McCormick Salt Free All Purpose
   Seasoning

McCormick Salt Free Garlic and Herb
Seasoning
McCormick Salt Free It's a Dilly
McCormick Salt Free Lemon and
Pepper Seasoning

Spices: The spices listed are acceptable in the brands that follow:

Allspice
Anise
Basil, Whole Sweet Basil
Bay Leaves, Select Whole Bay Leaves,
Ground Bay Leaves
Dehydrated Bell Pepper, Green Bell
Pepper Flakes
Celery Flakes, Celery Salt, Celery Seed
Mild and Hot Chili Powder, Dark Chili
Powder
Chives
Cilantro
Cinnamon, Ground Cinnamon,
Cinnamon Sticks
Cloves, Ground Cloves
Coriander
Cumin
Curry Powder
Dill Weed
Fennel, Fennel Seed
Crushed Garlic, Garlic Powder, Garlic
Salt, Granulated Garlic, Minced
Garlic, Parsleyed Garlic Salt
Ginger
Gumbo Filé
Marjoram
Mint, Mint Leaves
Mustard, Ground Mustard, Mustard
Seed, Yellow Mustard Seed
Nutmeg, Minced Nutmeg
Chopped Onion, Instant Diced Onions,
Minced Onion, Onion Powder,
Onion Salt, Chopped Green Onions,
Onion Juice

Oregano, Oregano Leaves, Oregano
Seeds
Paprika, Fancy Paprika
Parsley, Parsley Flakes, Italian Parsley
Black Pepper, Black Peppercorns,
Ground Red (Cayenne) Pepper,
Crushed Red Pepper, White Pepper
Pickling Spice
Poppy Seed
Rosemary
Sage, Ground Sage
Salt
Sesame Seeds
Tarragon
Thyme, Whole Thyme Leaves
Tumeric

Brand Names:

Astor
Breaux Mart
Deep South
Durkee
Food Club
Lawry's
Master Choice
McCormick
Morton & Bassett of San Francisco, All
Natural, No MSG, No Preservatives
Old Bay
Rex
Schilling
Shur Fine
Spice Island
Spice World
The Spice Hunter
Tone's
Trader's Choice
Valu Time
Whole Foods
Zatarain's

Soups & Broths

Bean Cuisine White Bean Soup
Bean Cuisine Black Bean Soup
Bean Cuisine Split Pea Soup
Bob's Red Mill Black Bean
Bob's Red Mill 13 Bean Soup Mix
Bootsie's South Louisiana Cooking Ten
   Bean Soup
Lysander's Black Bean Soup
 Mills Choice Bean Soup
Lysander's Great Northern Bean Soup
Da Vinci Escarole in Chicken Broth
   Canned Soup
"Imagine" Zesty Gazpacho
Da Vinci Lentil Canned Soup
Progresso Lentil Soup
Shariann's Spicy French Green Lentil
   Soup
Taste Adventure Curry Lentil Soup
Lysander's Minestrone Soup
Taste Adventure Golden Pea Soup
Shariann's Organic Tomato with
   Roasted Bell Pepper Soup
Shariann's Vegetarian French Onion
   Soup
Swanson's Beef Broth
Sweet Sue Beef Broth
Health Valley Fat-Free Beef Flavored
   Broth
Health Valley Chicken Broth
Shelton's Chicken Broth
Shelton's Chicken Broth with Salt &
   Spices
Arrowhead Mills Mushroom Broth

Spreads

Alouette Spreadable Cheeses: Vegetable
   Jardin Gourmet, Garlic & Herbs,
   Sundried Tomato and Basil
Athenos Feta Spread Original
Athenos Feta Spread Sun Dried Tomato
   & Basil
Goldy's Goumet Spreadable Cheeses:
   Roasted Pepper & Jalapeno Jack,
   Roasted Garlic With Fine Herbs,
   Sundried Tomato & Smoked
   Prozzarella
Baba Ganoush Eggplant & Tahini
   Spread
Colavita Peppazza Hot Pepper Spread
Morea Roasted Red Pepper Spread
Morea Feta & Sun Dried Tomato
   Spread
Schilling Garlic & Herb Spread
Schilling Quick & Easy Garlic Spread
Sun Fix Roma Italia Spread
Whole Foods Artichoke Bread Spread
Whole Foods Eggplant Bread Spread
Whole Foods Olive Bread Spread
Whole Foods Roasted Pepper Bread
   Spread

Syrup

Cary's Sugar Free Syrup
Spring Tree Sugar Free Syrup
Vermont Sugar Free Maple Syrup

Tahini

Marantha Natural Foods Sesame Tahini
Tribe of Two Shieks Sesame Tahini

Tapenades

California Harvest Artichoke Tapenade
California Harvest Green Olive
   Tapenade
California Harvest Kalamata Black
   Olive Tapenade
Olivier Napa Valley Mediterranean
   Kalamata Olive Sun-Dried Tomato
   Tapenade

California Harvest Portabello Mushroom Tapenade

California Harvest Red Bell Pepper Tapenade

California Harvest Sun-Dried Tomato Tapenade

Tofu

Frieda's Soft Tofu

Frieda's Firm Tofu

Galaxy Foods Veggie Shreds Cheddar Flavor Made With Tofu

House Organic Soft Tofu

Mori-Nu Tofu: Lite, Soft, Silken Firm, Extra Firm

Smoke & Fire Thai Smoked Tofu

Smoke & Fire Lemon Garlic Smoked Tofu

Soya Kaas Tofu: Jalapeno Mexi-Kaas, Mild Cheddar Style, Monterey Jack, Mozzarella Style

Tree of Life Baked Organic Tofu

White Wave Tofu: Fat Reduced, Firm, Extra Firm

White Wave Baked Organic Tofu Garlic Herb Italian Style

White Wave Baked Organic Tofu Seasame Peanut Thai

Whole Foods Tofu

Tomatoes, Canned and Sun-Dried

Sun-Dried

Bella Cucina Sun-Dried Tomatoes

Bella Sun Luci Sun-Dried Tomatoes

Boscoli Sun-Dried Tomatoes

Frieda's Marinated Dried Tomatoes

Gilroy Farms Marinated Sun-Dried Tomatoes

Melissa's Sun-Dried Tomatoes

Mezzetta's Sun-Dried Tomatoes

Moshe Pupik and Ali Mishmunken's Sun-Dried Tomatoes (Kosher)

Pelloponnese Sun-Dried Tomato Relish

Piaceri dall 'Orto Dry Tomatoes

Sonoma Marinated Dried Tomatoes

Sunsweet Marinated Dried Tomatoes

Canned

America's Choice Crushed Tomatoes

America's Choice Whole Tomatoes

Contadina Whole Tomatoes

Delchamps Whole Tomatoes, Peeled, Diced

Del Monte Fresh Cut Tomatoes

Food Club Diced Tomatoes

Food Club Whole Peeled Tomatoes

Hunt's Plain Diced Tomatoes

Hunt's Whole Tomatoes

L'Esprit de Compagne Virginia Sun-Ripened Tomatoes

Kuner's Chili Tomates

Kuner's Tomatoes & Jalapenos

Luigi Vitelli Italian Peeled Tomatoes

Master Choice Whole Tomatoes

Millina's Finest Tomatoes

Muir Glen Organic Diced Tomatoes with and without Seasonings

Muir Glen Organic Ground Peeled Tomatoes

Muir Glen Organic Peeled Tomatoes

Pastene Tomatoes

Pomi Chopped Tomatoes

Pomi Strained Tomatoes

Pomodora Fresca Solo Fresh Plum Tomatoes - Cayenne Hot

Pomodora Fresca Solo Fresh Plum Tomatoes Preserved in Own Juices with Vinegar

Progresso Peeled Tomatoes with Basil

Progresso Peeled Tomatoes

Progresso Crushed Tomatoes

Roberts Big R Tomatoes

Rotel Mild Whole Tomato and Green Chilies
Rotel Extra Hot Whole Tomatoes and Green Chilies
Rotel Diced Tomatoes and Green Chilies
S&W Tomatoes-all varieties
Shur Fine Diced Tomatoes
Shur Fine Whole Peeled Tomatoes
6 in 1 Whole Ground Tomatoes
Thrifty Maid Tomatoes
Thrifty Maid Diced Tomatoes
Thrifty Maid Whole Tomatoes
Whole Foods Whole Peeled Organic Tomatoes

Tomato - Sauces, Paste, Purée
Sauces
The Grower's Co. Nouvelle Garni Selection Dried Tomato Sauce and Seasoning Concentrate
America's Choice Tomato Sauce
Amore Tomato Sauce
Barilla Tomato Sauce - Sweet Pepper and Garlic
Cento Tomato Sauce
Delchamps Tomato Sauce
Don Pomodoro Tomato and Basil Sauce
El Pato Tomato Sauce
Millina's Finest Tomato Sauce
Food Club Tomato Sauce
Muir Glen Organic Chunky Tomato Sauce
Paladini Cioppino Sauce
Paladini Tomato-Basil Sauce
Patsy's Tomato Sauce with Olives and Capers
Pomodoro Fresca ANA Fresh Plum Tomatoes and Seasonings
Rustichella D'Abruzzo Tomato Sauce

Sal and Judy's Original Recipe Tomato Sauce
Shur Fine Tomato Sauce
Thrify Maid Tomato Sauce
Whole Foods 365 Tomato Sauce
Paste and Purée
America's Choice Tomato Purée
Amore Concentrated Sun-Dried Tomato Paste
Amore Concentrated Sun-Dried Tomato-Garlic Paste
Centro Tomato Paste
Contadina Tomato Paste
Del Monte Tomato Paste
Montahi Tomato Paste
Muir Glen Organic Tomato Paste
Progresso Tomato Paste
Progresso Tomato Purée
Thrifty Maid Tomato Paste
Whole Foods 365 Tomato Purée
Whole Foods Puree Organic Tomatoes

Vegetables, Canned
Cora Mia Artichoke Hearts
Cohevi Artichoke Hearts
Del Destino Hearts of Artichoke
Haddon House Artichoke Bottoms
Haddon House Artichoke Hearts
Pesto Artichokes
Prestige Artichoke Hearts
Progresso Artichoke Hearts
Reese Artichoke Hearts
Reese Artichoke Salad
Roland Artichoke Hearts
Romanina Artichoke Hearts
Romanina Artichoke Hearts, Quartered
S&W Artichoke Hearts
Vigo Artichoke Hearts
Del Monte Asparagus Spears
Del Monte Fresh Cut Asparagus Tips
Food Club Asparagus

Green Giant Asparagus Spears
Le Sueur Asparagus Spears
Pepita Moreno Asparagus
Pride Asparagus
Pride Asparagus Spears
Reese Asparagus
Reese Asparagus Spears
Shur Fine Asparagus
Thank You Asparagus Spears
Thrifty Maid Asparagus
Walla Walla Asparagus
Whopper Walla Walla Colossal Extra
　　Long White Asparagus
Chun King Bamboo Shoots
Dynasty Bamboo Shoots
La Choy Sliced Bamboo Shoots
Port Arthur Bamboo Shoots
Chun King Bean Sprouts
La Choy Bean Sprouts
Ty Ling Bean Sprouts
Chun King Water Chestnuts
La Choy Water Chestnuts
Port Arthur Water Chestnuts
Ty Ling Water Chestnuts
Bush's Chopped Collard Greens
Stubb's Harvest Collard Greens
Bush's Mustard Greens
Stubb's Harvest Mustard Greens
The Allen's Sunshine Turnip Greens
Bush's Turnip Greens
Food Club Turnip Greens
Stubb's Harvest Turnip Greens
Bosco Garlic
CheRith Valley Gardens Hearts of Palm
Maria Hearts of Palm
Haddon House Hearts of Palm
Reese Hearts of Palm
Regency Hearts of Palm
Roland Hearts of Palm
Stubb's Kale
America's Choice Mushrooms

B in B Mushrooms
Flavorite Mushrooms
Food Club Mushrooms
Giorgio Pieces and Stems Mushrooms
Green Giant Mushrooms
Kame Straw Mushrooms
Roland Mushrooms
Thrifty Maid Mushrooms
Ty Ling Stir Fry Mushrooms
Stubbs Cut Okra
Trappey's Cut Okra
Trappey's Cut Okra and Tomato
The Allens Popeye Brand Chopped
　　Spinach
America's Choice Leaf Spinach
Del Monte Fresh Cut Whole Leaf
　　Spinach
Fresh Cut Spinach
Pesto Spinach
Bruce's Sliced Squash
CheRith Valley Gardens Sunburst
　　Squash
Witt's Vegetable Garnish

Vegetables, Frozen

Haddon House Artichoke Hearts and
　　Bottoms
Dixiana Asparagus Spears
America's Choice Broccoli
Astor Broccoli
Cascade Farms Broccoli
Dixiana Broccoli
McKenzie's Broccoli
Shur Fine Broccoli
Thrifty Maid Broccoli
America's Choice Brussel Sprouts
Astor Brussel Sprouts
McKenzie's Brussel Sprouts
Thrifty Maid Brussel Sprouts
Astor Butter Beans
Dixiana Butter Beans

McKenzie's Butter Beans
Astor Cauliflower
America's Choice Green Beans
Bird's Eye Side Orders Green Beans
    with Almonds
C&W Green Beans
Dixiana Green Beans
Food Club Green Beans
Shur Fine Green Beans
Sno Pac Green Beans
Thrifty Maid Green Beans
Whole Foods 365 Cut Green Beans
Dixiana Collard Greens
Food Club Collard Greens
Dixiana Mustard Greens
McKenzie's Mustard Greens
Dixiana Turnip Greens
Food Club Turnip Greens
McKenzie's Turnip Greens
America's Choice Lima Beans
Astor Lima Beans
Food Club Lima Beans
McKenzie's Lima Beans
Thrifty Maid Lima Beans
Bird's Eye Frozen Foods
Cascadian Farm Frozen Vegetables:
    Broccoli, Cut Green Beans, Organic
    Garden Peas, Chopped Spinach
Green Giant Frozen Foods
Janet Lee Brand
Pic Sweet Frozen Foods
Dixiana Chopped Green Peppers
Food Club Chopped Green Peppers
America's Choice Okra
Dixiana Okra
Food Club Okra
McKenzie's Okra
McKenzie's Okra, Tomatoes and
    Onions
Thrifty Maid Okra
Dixiana Onions
Dixiana Black Eyed Peas

McKenzie's Black Eyed Peas
Astor Peas
Cascade Farms Peas
C&W Petite Peas
Dixiana Peas
Food Club Crowder Peas
Food Club Green Peas
McKenzie's Petite Peas
McKenzie's Peas
Shur Fine Green Peas
Sno Pac Green Peas
La Choy Snow Pea Pods
Thrifty Maid Peas
Whole Foods 365 Green Peas
America's Choice Spinach
Astor Spinach
Cascade Farms Spinach
Food Club Spinach
McKenzie's Spinach
Shur Fine Spinach
Sno Pac Spinach
Dixiana Seasonings
Chef's Seasonings
McKenzie's Seasoning Blend

Vegetables: Gourmet, Marinated, and Pickled

Reese's Marinated Artichoke Hearts
Reese's Artichoke Salad
America's Choice Sauerkraut
Bubbies Sauerkraut
Cascadian Farms Sauerkraut
Clausen's Sauerkraut
Cosmic Cabbage Sauerkraut
Del Monte Sauerkraut
Eden Organic Sauerkraut
Kruegermann Sauerkraut
Vlasic Sauerkraut
Cara Mia Marinated Mushrooms
DaVinci Marinated Mushrooms
Gogliano's Gourmet Marinated
    Mushrooms
Epicurean Specialty Gourmet Dried
    Mushrooms and Peppers
Boscoli Asparagus
Cara Mia Marinated Asparagus
Cara Mia Marinated Artichoke Crowns
    & Hearts
Progresso Marinated Artichoke Hearts
Italbrand Quartered & Marinated
    Artichoke Hearts
Tutto Calabria Stuffed Aubergines
Mezzetta Pickled Broccoli
Cara Mia Marinated Brussels Sprouts
Mezzetta Pickled Brussel Sprouts
Mezzetta's Pickled Cauliflower
Tutto Calabria Roasted Fennel
Boscoli Green Beans
Porter's Pick a Dilly Farmstyle Dilly
    Beans
Porter's Pick a Dilly Farmstyle Dilly
    Beans - Great Garlic
Porter's Pick a Dilly Farmstyle Dilly
    Beans - Mild
Rapazzini Spiced Beans

Sonoma Muffaletta Dried Tomato and
    Olive Relish
Wickland Farms Blue Lake Spiced
    Beans
Boscoli Garlic
CheRith Valley Gardens Pickled Garlic
Mezzetta Pickled Crushed Garlic
Well-Pac Pickled Ginger
Reese's Marinated Hearts of Palm
Volcano Valley Sliced and Marinated
    Hearts of Palm
Boscoli Italian Olive Salad
CheRith Valley Gardens Pickled Okra
Talk O'Texas Crisp Okra Pickles
Tiffe's Pickled Okra
Mezzetta Pickled Okra
Boscoli Onions
Bruno's Market Cocktail Onions
Gordon Award Picled Onions
Holland Pickled Onions
Mezzetta Pickled Onions
Reese Pickled Onions
Star Imported Onions
Star Imported Pepperoncini
Batampte Pickled Tomatoes

Vinegar

Antica Acetaia Dei Carandini Balsamic
    Vinegar of Modena
Belle Cucina Cabernet Vinegar
Blue Runner Vinegar
California Harvest Vinegars
Candoni Balsamic Vinegar
Cento Garlic Flavored Wine Vinegar
DaVinci Vinegar
De Nign's Wine Vinegar
Eden Selected Red Wine Vinegar
Food Club Vinegar
Grey Poupon Imported Balsamic
    Vinegar of Modena
Heinz Distilled White Wine Vinegar

Herbs de Provence Provencal Vinegar
Master Choice Vinegar
Monari Federzoni Red Wine Vinegar
Monari Federzoni White Wine Vinegar
Pastene Imported Balsamic Vinegar of
   Modena
Progresso's White Wine Vinegar
Reese Garlic Flavored Wine Vinegar
Reese Maitre Jacques Garlic Wine Vinegar
Regina Red Wine Vinegar
Regina Red Wine Vinegar with Garlic
Regina White Wine Vinegar
Regina White Wine Vinegar with
   Tarragon
Spice Island Vinegar
Star Italian Kitchen Vinegar
Spectrum Naturals Vinegars
Stonewall Kitchen Chili Chive Vinegar
S&W Vinegar
Whole Foods Champagne Vinegar
Whole Foods Red Wine Vinegar
Zatarain's White Wine Vinegar

Yogurt
Breyers Yogurt, Sugar Free
Brown Cow Farm Yogurt, Sugar Free
Continental Non-Fat Yogurt
Dannon Yogurt, Sugar Free
Horizon Organic Yogurt, Sugar Free:
   Plain and Non-Fat
Mountain High Natural Fat Free Plain
   Yogurt
Nancy's Organic Yogurt
Nancy's Organic Low-Fat Yogurt
Nancy's Organic Non-Fat Yogurt
Natural Alta Dena Select Yogurt, Sugar
   Free
Pavel's Original Russian Yogurt
Pavel's Low-Fat Russian Yogurt
Pavel's Non-Fat Russian Yogurt
Stonyfield Farm Plain Non-Fat Yogurt
Straws Family Creamery Plain Yogurt

INDEX

- Appleton, Nancy, PhD., *Lick The Sugar Habit,* Santa Monica, Avery Publishing Group, 1996.

- http://www.anndeweesallencom/
  (Ann de Wees Allen, N.D., Glycemic Research Institute)

- http://www.caloriecontrol.org
  (Calorie Control Council)

- http://www.cdc.gov/nccdphp/ddt/facts.html
  (Diabetes)

- http://www.geocities.com/HotSprings/4582/
  (Marcel Bovy, The Montignac Method, Food for Thought)

- Guyton, Arthur C., M.D., John E. Hall, Ph. D., *The Textbook on Medical Physiology,* Philadelphia: W.B. Saunders, 1996.

- http://www.lanr.unl.edu/pubs/foods/g1030.htm
  (University of Nebraska NebGuide, "Sweeteners")

- http://lifelines.com/libry2.html
  (Lifelines Health Science and Research Library)

- http://www.mendosa.com/glfactor.html
  (The GI Factor)

- http://www.montignac.com/en/gindex.html
  (Glycaemic Index Table)

- Montignac Michel, *Dine Out and Lose Weight,* Paris: Artulen, 1991.

- Montignac, Michel, *Eat Yourself Slim,* Paris: Artulen, 1991.

- http://www.smartbasic.com/glos.news/3glyc.index.dec93.html
  (Smart Basic Intelliscope)

- Steward, Bethea, Andrew, Balart, *SugarBusters!™ Cut Sugar to Trim Fat,* Metairie: 1995.

- http://www.sunflower.org/~cfsdays/nutrasweet.html
  ("The Not So Sweet News About NutraSweet")

- http://www.tiac.net/users/mgold/aspartame2/adverse-new.txt
  (Aspartame Toxicity Information Center)

- Tordoff MG, Alleva AM, Effect of drinking soda sweetened with aspartame or high-fructose, corn syrup on food intake and body weight. *American Journal of Clinical Nutrition,* 1990;51:963-969.

- http://wctc.net/~tbart/NutraSweet.html
  (Untitled)

Order Form

Please send

_____ copies of *SUGAR BUST FOR LIFE!...WITH THE BRENNANS,*
                    Part II at $14.95 each $_____

_____ copies of *ORIGINAL SUGAR BUST FOR LIFE!...WITH THE BRENNANS*
                              at $14.95 each $_____

               plus $3.75 postage and handling for one copy $_____

               add $1.50 postage for each additional book $_____

               Orleans Parish residents add $1.35 each
                    (9% city and state sales tax) $_____

               Louisiana state residents add $0.60 each
                    (4% state sales tax only) $_____

                              TOTAL $_____

Mail my *Sugar Bust For Life!...With The Brennans* book(s) to:

Name: _____

Address: _____

City/State/Zip: _____

Phone: _____

Make checks payable to:
SUGAR BUST FOR LIFE!...WITH THE BRENNANS/Shamrock Publishing
Charge to (check one):
☐ VISA   ☐ MasterCard   ☐ American Express   ☐ Discover

Account Number: _____ Expiration Date: _____

Signature: _____

Mail to: *SUGAR BUST FOR LIFE!...WITH THE BRENNANS*
                  c/o Shamrock Publishing
                  P.O. Box 15439
                  New Orleans, LA 70175-5439

Phone Orders: 504-897-6770 or
                  Fax: 504-897-6770

E-mail: SBforL@aol.com